South Wales

Car Tours

Roger Thomas

Acknowledgements
Many thanks to Heather Pearson at the Ordnance Survey for checking
the routes.

Front cover photograph: *Carreg Cennen Castle, near Llandeilo*
Title page photograph: *Cardiff Castle*

Author: Roger Thomas
Series Editor: Anne-Marie Edwards
Editors: Donald Greig, Nicola Gadsby
Designers: Brian Skinner, Ellen Moorcraft
Photographs: Wales Tourist Board and Jarrold Publishing

Jarrold Publishing   ISBN 0-7117-0846-0

First published 1996 by Ordnance Survey and Jarrold Publishing

Ordnance Survey   Jarrold Publishing
Romsey Road   Whitefriars
Maybush   Norwich NR3 1TR
Southampton SO16 4GU

Printed in Great Britain by Jarrold Book Printing, Thetford, Norfolk 1/96

CONTENTS

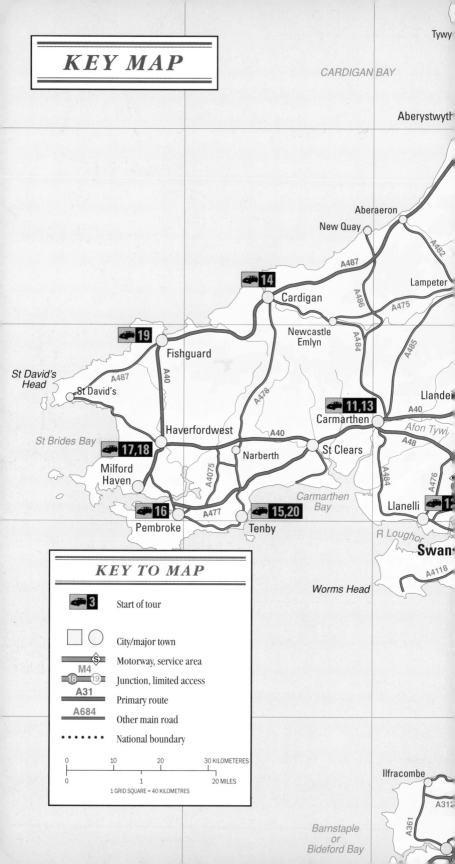

INTRODUCTION TO SOUTH WALES

This region is, without doubt, one of the most challenging in Wales to characterise. It does not easily evoke a single strong image. North Wales is dominated by the mountains of Snowdonia. Central Wales is quintessential green farming country. But the south? South Wales is noted for its variety, not for its uniformity. Within its boundaries – which stretch for well over 100 miles from the Welsh border to Pembrokeshire in the far south-west – South Wales includes a surprising degree of scenic diversity.

Its two national parks could not be more different. The Brecon Beacons park consists of high, grassy mountains which roll, wave-like, across the landscape. Pembrokeshire, on the other hand, is famous for its coastline, one of the finest stretches of coastal natural beauty in Europe.

Similarly, South Wales's two official 'Areas of Outstanding Natural Beauty' have little in common. The Gower Peninsula is a promontory of sandy bays and spectacular headlands, while the Wye Valley between Chepstow and Monmouth is flanked by steep, thickly wooded hills. Other pieces in South Wales's jumbled jigsaw include the former industrial valleys, the pastoral Vale of Glamorgan, the cliff-backed Glamorgan Heritage Coast, the sands of Carmarthen Bay, the traditional farmlands around Carmarthen itself, and the lovely Teifi Valley. Piece them all together and you have a portrait of an area of great and fascinating variety.

Likewise, there is not a lot of common ground between Cardiff and, say, Carmarthen. Cardiff, Wales's capital, is at the hub of commercial and industrial Wales. Well over half of Wales's population of 2³/4 million live in the south-east, concentrated in a band between Swansea, Cardiff and Newport. In the wake of the old heavy industries based on coal and metal, new high-tech companies have moved into this south-eastern belt. The cities and towns here now deal in administration, financial services and other white-collar work, where once they served the coal, iron and steel industries. Moreover, overseas companies have moved in, adding to an already

Cardiff's splendid Civic Centre

The green hills and mountains of the Brecon Beacons National Park

cosmopolitan cultural mix focused around Cardiff.

The further west you travel, the more traditional and unchanging Wales becomes. Around Carmarthen, the farming communities go about their business much as they have always done, EC regulations notwithstanding. Go to the weekly livestock market in Carmarthen, or Newcastle Emlyn, or Llandovery, and you will hear the Welsh language in everyday use. Yet you will be lucky to come across a Welsh speaker while shopping in Cardiff or Newport.

A trip along the A40, one of South Wales's main through routes, provides a good indication of the way in which traditional Wales asserts itself gradually the further west you travel. Around Abergavenny and Crickhowell less than 5 per cent of the population speak Welsh. This rises to 10 per cent around Brecon, 30 per cent at Sennybridge, and about 60 per cent around Carmarthen.

So South Wales is a mixed bag of influences; scenic, social and cultural. Yet it is possible to draw up certain ground rules as guidelines for bemused visitors. If you like mountains, head for the Brecon Beacons. For countryside with a more gentle touch, try the Wye, Usk or Teifi valleys, or the Vale of Glamorgan, or the farmlands around Carmarthen. For art, architecture and contemporary culture, Cardiff offers a rich menu which reflects its status as a capital city of international repute. An hour's drive from urban South Wales will take you to away-from-it-all country towns and villages where the traditional values of rural life still hold sway. Along the coast, there is yet more choice. For pure coastal scenery at its natural best, Pembrokeshire and the Gower Peninsula are hard to beat. Carmarthen Bay is renowned for its long, sandy beaches, Barry Island and Porthcawl are the places to go for bright and breezy seaside resorts, while between the two are the remote cliffs of the Glamorgan Heritage Coast.

Two National Parks

The mountainous heart of South Wales is to be found in the Brecon Beacons National Park. Its 519 square miles roll westwards from the Wales–England border to the country town of Llandeilo north of Swansea. The park contains four distinct mountain ranges – and it is here that the confusion begins. The Brecon Beacons themselves stand in the centre of the park, rising almost 3,000 feet (914 m) to the summit of Pen y Fan, the highest peak in South Wales. East of the Beacons, along the border, are the Black Mountains, while the park's western landscapes consist of the high moors of Fforest Fawr and the Black Mountain (singular!).

Most walkers head for the central Beacons or the Black Mountains. The great attraction for walkers here is the wide, open spaces. But these can also represent danger, for the weather can change suddenly in the Beacons, and those grassy mountain slopes that looked so inviting can quickly turn into misty, windy and inhospitable uplands with precious little in the way of shelter from penetrating conditions. Always make sure that you are well equipped if tackling the exhilarating high routes which these mountains have to offer. Other leisure opportunities in the Brecon Beacons include pony trekking, canal cruising, canoeing and pot holing, the latter in the limestone country along the southern rim of the park.

The Pembrokeshire Coast National Park stretches for 180 miles from Amroth (near Tenby) in the south to Poppit Sands (near Cardigan) in the north. Pembrokeshire was known as *Gwlad Hud a Lledrith* ('The Land of Magic and Enchantment') in the early folk tales of Wales. Today's visitors feel much the same about Pembrokeshire's wonderful coastal scenery and prolific wildlife. The park contains a variety of coastal scenery. In the south there are sandy beaches and towering limestone cliffs. Along the sheltered waters of the Milford Haven wooded creeks wind their way inland. West-facing Pembrokeshire along St Bride's Bay has more sands and sea-cliffs, whilst the northern coast is rocky and indented. The boundaries of the park hug the coastline in a narrow band, dipping inland only once to encompass the Preseli Hills, a moorland range dotted with prehistoric sites.

Most of the holiday accommodation is based around Tenby and Saundersfoot in the south. Other parts of the park are served by small places like Dale, Broad Haven, St David's and Newport, where it is easy to get away from it all, even in the height of summer. This especially applies if you are prepared to walk along a stretch of the long-distance Pembrokeshire Coast Path. Often, you will not have to go far to find a headland, cove, or sometimes a complete beach, all to yourself.

Historic Landscapes

The varied terrain in South Wales has, in many ways, moulded the region's history. In medieval times, Norman invaders stuck mainly to the strategic lower ground when constructing their chain of castles to control the native Welsh. More than a millennium earlier, Iron Age man had different ideas, preferring the natural defences afforded by hillforts built in more mountainous terrain. There is plentiful evidence of both types of stronghold in South Wales, along with reminders of prehistoric ritual, Roman invasion and consolidation, early Christian shrines, and the area's relatively recent – and remarkable – industrial past.

Walking along the Pembrokeshire Coast Path

Prehistoric settlement and the coming of the Romans

In the dim past, prehistoric man constructed stone chambers – known as *cromlechs* – for the communal burial of the dead. Outstanding examples of these in South Wales include Pentre Ifan in Pembrokeshire's Preseli Hills and Tinkinswood in the Vale of Glamorgan near Cardiff. The sense of mystery surrounding these ancient monuments is further heightened by the discovery that Preseli's 'bluestones', of which Pentre Ifan is constructed, also went into the making of Stonehenge on distant Salisbury Plain.

In the remote wastes of the Brecon Beacons there are lone standing stones like Maen Llwyd and Maen Llia, which may have been markers for early travellers. And crowning many hilltops are the remnants of Iron Age forts dating from around 600 BC, relative newcomers compared to the stone monuments of our early ancestors. These sturdy hillforts were built by local Celtic tribes. If you walk up to Crug Hywel ('Howell's Fort') on the steep hill above Crickhowell, you will see how its builders made good use of a strong, flat-topped defensive site which drops away sharply into the valley.

The Romans turned their attentions to South Wales 2,000 years ago, conquering the area by AD 74–78. They controlled the native tribes by constructing a network of strongholds linked by well-engineered roads. The Sarn Helen Roman Road between their forts at Neath and Brecon still exists in parts. Other Roman settlements included Cardiff, Caerwent and Carmarthen, the latter their most westerly fort in Britain.

The Romans' most notable site was at Caerleon, where they stationed 6,000 elite legionary troops in a major stronghold complete with an amphitheatre and bath-house complex. Some historians attribute the Romans' interest in South Wales to the search for gold. They found it deep in the hills at Pumsaint, where they established the only known Roman gold mine in Britain.

Tinkinswood Burial Chamber, in the Vale of Glamorgan

The 'Age of Saints'

The Romans departed at the end of the fourth century, their empire in ruins. By the sixth century, Celtic saints like St Illtyd and St David, Wales's patron saint, had began to spread the Christian message in Wales. During this 'Age of Saints', these dynamic missionaries travelled widely, founding monasteries and religious centres at places like Llantwit Major and St David's, where today's cathedral stands on a site of David's original community.

Caerphilly Castle, one of Europe's finest surviving medieval fortresses

The Norman Conquest

The Normans arrived in England in 1066, and soon turned their attentions to South Wales. The Welsh had no convincing answer to the forces led by William FitzOsbern, one of William the Conqueror's most accomplished lieutenants. Military success was consolidated by the construction of a string of castles (see box feature). Over the next few centuries, many of these castles were extended and improved. Mighty Caerphilly Castle – 'Giant Caerffili' according to a medieval Welsh poet – is the most impressive of them all. This massive castle, with its water defences and formidable series of walls within walls, represents a high point of medieval military architecture. The newcomers to South Wales also spread their influence by establishing fortified towns around many of their castles. At Tenby and Pembroke, for example, you can still see well-preserved stretches of medieval town walls.

Castles through the ages

Wales is known as a 'land of castles'. Hundreds of fortifications dot the landscape, some no more than earthen mounds, others still standing, their powerful presence undimmed by the passage of time. South Wales can claim a significant 'first' in the history of castle building. Up until the middle of the eleventh century, castles were rudimentary motte-and-bailey fortifications consisting of earthen mounds defended by timber stockades. It was the Normans who made an enormous advance in castle engineering when they built the first stone castle in Britain at Chepstow. Their stranglehold over South Wales was achieved through an ambitious castle-building programme which saw fortresses constructed at strategic points from Chepstow on the border to Pembroke in South-west Wales. Indeed, the Normans seem to have paid special attention to South Wales, for the remains of about 80 stone castles can be seen here – more than in any other part of Britain.

To this stock of castles we can add the 'sham' mansions built by the wealthy magnates of the Industrial Revolution. Merthyr Tydfil's Cyfarthfa Castle, with its mock battlements, reflects the power and authority of the new nineteenth-century barons who ruled the iron industry. Cardiff Castle's breathtaking opulence is directly attributable to the incredible fortunes generated at the coal-exporting docklands – though in this case, the nineteenth-century 'castle' can at least claim some authenticity since it was constructed on the site of a Roman camp and Norman keep.

Industrial times

The relatively recent history of South Wales has strong links with Britain's Industrial Revolution. Despite the 'How Green Was My Valley' image under which South Wales – unfairly – still labours, coalmining was not the only industrial activity there. Neither was it the first. Long before the advent of the Industrial Revolution proper and large-scale coalmining, South Wales was an established and innovative centre for metal production.

From the mid-eighteenth century, the coincidence of iron ore, limestone and coal – the three ingredients for ironmaking – turned Merthyr Tyfdil into the 'iron capital of the world' and Wales's largest town. The first of the great ironworks was built at Dowlais, a district of Merthyr, in 1759. Other blast furnaces were set up in neighbouring towns along the northern rim of the South Wales valleys, while South-west Wales around Llanelli specialised in tinplate and Swansea established itself as a copper-producing centre.

Coal was not fully exploited until the nineteenth century. One area in particular – the Rhondda – become synonymous with the so-called 'black gold'. Coalmines were sunk all the way along the narrow valleys of the Rhondda Fawr ('Big') and Fach ('Little'), any spare space within the confines of the valley floors being taken up by the tightly packed terraced housing hastily built to accommodate a burgeoning workforce. Pit village merged with pit village to create a continuous industrial development in what had previously been an untouched rural landscape.

With coal came communications. Railway lines fanned out from Cardiff and Newport into the valleys, bringing the coal to booming docklands for shipment. Cardiff grew up on the back of the coal trade from a small coastal settlement to a major sea port, and in the early twentieth century, just before the bubble burst, it became the world's busiest coal-exporting port.

ENJOY YOUR TOUR

Before you set off, please read though the tour to get an idea of the route. If the visibility is poor, it might be better to leave the higher routes through the Brecon Beacons National Park for another day. The weather in the Beacons is fickle and fast-changing; one day can be wet and misty, the next bright and clear. Pick a good day, and you will enjoy the views and the walking opportunities outlined in the routes to their full.

Eighteen of the 20 tours are circular, so they can be started at any point. To make the routes easier to follow, all navigational instructions have been printed in bold. The route descriptions also contain boxed letters which tie in with those on the map. Their purpose is to aid navigation and, in many instances, highlight sections of the route requiring particular attention. The times given for each tour cover the motoring element only, based on a relaxed pace. In most cases, you will find that the tour takes a full day if you stop off at the places and attractions described, or follow any of the walks mentioned. If you plan more extensive walks the Pathfinder guides or the Pathfinder maps at 1:25 000 (2 inches to 1 mile/4cm to 1km) are ideal – for details see the inside back cover.

Please note that opening times for the various attractions may have changed since going to press, so it is advisable to telephone before visiting. Inevitably, we have had to condense some of the more complicated and lengthy opening details. Generally speaking, when an attraction states that it is closed on Mondays, it will be open for Bank Holidays. Similarly, most places will be closed over the Christmas period even when it is stated that they are open throughout the year.

There are no major problems attached to driving in Wales. You will find that many of the routes are refreshingly traffic-free, apart from peak summer weekends and Bank Holidays. Keep an eye open for sheep though, especially on minor mountain roads. They are unpredictable animals who always seem to do the wrong thing when a car approaches! In Pembrokeshire in particular, some minor roads are lined with high hedges which severely restrict visibility, so take extra care. If you are sightseeing on any single-track road, pull over as often as possible to allow following traffic to pass.

THE WYE VALLEY AND VALE OF USK

61 MILES – 3 HOURS
START AND FINISH AT CHEPSTOW

Two outstandingly beautiful river valleys, the Wye and the Usk, define much of this route. Wales's border country, quiet and undisturbed today, has a history of war and conflict. A natural gateway into Wales, the area was settled by Roman conquerors and Norman barons, whose strongholds can still be seen. Caerleon boasts some of Britain's finest Roman remains, and the route is dotted with medieval castles large and small. As well as taking you through an historic landscape, this tour travels through wonderful walking country with – especially in the Wye Valley – many opportunities to follow waymarked trails.

Leave Chepstow town centre following signs to Monmouth and the A466. The road northwards passes Chepstow Racecourse, Wales's premier horse-racing venue and location of a huge open-air Sunday market which attracts traders and shoppers from far and wide.

The road between Chepstow and Monmouth travels through the part of the Wye Valley officially classified as an 'Area of Outstanding Natural Beauty'. Thick woodlands line a narrow valley carved by the winding Wye, and there are many scenic stopping-off places en route from which you can admire the view.

After the village of St Arvans, the road climbs up past Lover's Leap (on your right) to Wynd Cliff (on your left). Park the car here and follow the path through a woodland nature reserve to the breathtaking Eagle's Nest viewpoint 700 feet (213 m) above the valley, with views southwards over a huge horseshoe bend in the Wye and the Severn Estuary.

You can make your way down the cliff from here by the celebrated 365 Steps to Lower Wynd Cliff – but don't forget that you have to walk up again!

Continue along the A466 and shortly you will come to Tintern. This popular spot, always busy in summer, is famous for its Cistercian abbey (Cadw-Welsh Historic Monuments). It is also a good walking centre, with a variety of trails leading along the valley and through the woods. On the ridge above is the long-

· PLACES OF INTEREST ·

Chepstow
Set in a beautiful riverside landscape, this ancient gateway town to Wales has in its time been a strategic centre and marketplace. The town's mighty castle, set on a high bluff commanding the River Wye, was built as a stronghold for the Norman conquest of South-east Wales. Its eleventh-century Great Tower has the distinction of being the earliest stone castle in Britain. Over the following centuries, the defences were gradually extended, giving today's military historians an invaluable insight into the evolution of castle architecture. Open summer daily 9.30–6.30, winter Monday–Saturday 9.30–4, Sunday 11–4. Telephone: (01291) 624065.

Chepstow's medieval town walls enclose narrow streets. Its High Street is straddled by a well-preserved thirteenth-century town gate. The local museum, housed in an elegant eighteenth-century town house near the castle, reveals the town's rich and varied past. Open July–September, Monday–Saturday 10.30–1, 2–5.30. October–June, Monday–Saturday 11–1, 2–5, Sunday 2–5. Telephone: (01291) 625981. Two long-distance walks begin at Chepstow: the Wye Valley Walk, running for 52 miles to Hereford, and the Offa's Dyke Path, which follows a borderland route for 168 miles to Prestatyn on the North Wales coast.

Tintern Abbey

Monmouth's historic Monnow bridge

the eighth-century earthwork erected by King Offa of Mercia as the first official border between England and Wales (at Tintern, the current border is marked by the river).

The road northwards faithfully follows the course of the Wye, with glorious views of green riverbank and lush woodland. At Bigsweir Bridge, you cross for a short distance into England, entering Wales again at Redbrook.

On the approach to Monmouth, cross the river bridge A, go straight across the A40 at the traffic lights and drive into the centre of town. Follow the road along the main street and cross the

distance Offa's Dyke Path, which runs from near Chepstow all the way to Prestatyn in North Wales, a distance of over 170 miles. The path follows, wherever possible,

narrow medieval Monnow Bridge, turning right on to the B4233 at the roundabout immediately after.

Drive north-westwards

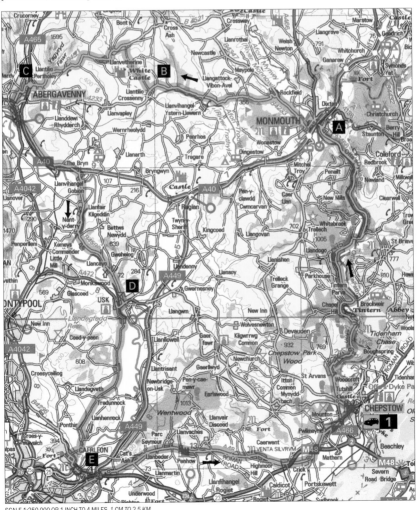

then westwards along the **B4233 via Rockfield.** Music fans will be familiar with this peaceful village as the home of a recording studio used by many famous bands and artists. The quiet B4233 travels through forgotten border country which is reminiscent of the gentle landscapes of rural France. It is all the more attractive thanks to the fast dual-carriageway A40 to the south, which takes nearly all the traffic into Wales from Monmouth.

Turn right on to the minor road on the approach to Llantilio Crosseny B, following the signs for White Castle (Cadw-Welsh Historic Monuments). (Llantilio Crosseny, incidentally, is home to a well-regarded music festival held in early summer.)

• PLACES OF INTEREST •

Tintern

Tintern and its romantic ruined abbey have been firm favourites with visitors since the early days of tourism. Poet William Wordsworth was moved to write a famous sonnet, *Lines composed a few miles above Tintern Abbey*, which perfectly expressed the romantic view of the landscape. The abbey, standing in an idyllic setting, continues to inspire strong emotions. It was founded by the Cistercians in 1131, and had an active life right up to the Dissolution of the Monasteries by Henry VIII in 1536. The industrious Cistercians turned Tintern into an important agricultural as well as religious centre. Although in ruin, their abbey has a rare grace, thanks to its location and the wealth of well-preserved detail – especially the tracery in the windows – still evident in its roofless shell. Open summer daily 9.30–6.30, winter Monday–Saturday 9.30–4, Sunday 11–4. Telephone: (01291) 689251.

The Victorian railway station at Tintern has undergone an imaginative transformation to become a visitor information centre. A varied choice of walks start from here. Open April–October daily 10.30–5.30. Telephone: (01291) 689566.

Monmouth

This gateway town has almost too much history. Two of its most famous sons, Henry V and Charles Stewart Rolls (of Rolls-Royce) are honoured by statues in Agincourt Square, a handsome open area lined with shops, inns and the eighteenth-century Shire Hall. The ruins of the castle in which Henry was born can be seen just off the Square, while a little further along the street Admiral Lord Nelson's life and times are recalled in the Nelson Collection, part of the excellent Monmouth Museum. The long main street, which bears evidence of the town's fashionable Georgian era, ends at Monnow Bridge, a narrow fortified gateway built to protect the western approaches and reputedly the only one of its kind in Britain. Monmouth's livestock markets are held on Mondays and Fridays, with general markets on Fridays and Saturdays.

White Castle, near Llantilio Crosseny

The flattish borderlands east of Abergavenny, with little in the way of natural defences, were vulnerable to attack. White Castle was one of the 'Three Castles of Gwent' (the others are at Grosmont and Skenfrith) built by the Normans to control their newly won territories. Its name derives from the fact that the stone walls would once have been covered with white plaster. Dating mainly from the twelfth and thirteenth centuries, it is the best preserved of the three, with sturdy walls, towers and gatehouse and deep moat still filled with water. Open April– September, daily 10–6. Telephone: (01873) 821252.

Abergavenny

Please see description in Tour 4.

Caerleon

It is a little-known fact that Caerleon ranks with Chester and York as one of the Romans' most important bases in Britain. Caerleon – *Isca* to the Romans, named after the River Usk – was one of their trio of fortress settlements. It was a complete town covering 50 acres (20

hectares), with barracks, an amphitheatre and lavish bath-house complex, the Romans' equivalent to today's leisure centre. The town, dating from AD 74, was built to accommodate the Second Augusta Legion, crack troops sent to Wales to defeat the local tribe known an the Silures. Extensive excavations have revealed a well-preserved amphitheatre, an oval arena in which combat and blood sports took place witnessed by 6,000 spectators. The foundations of a large barracks can also be seen, the only legionary barracks on view anywhere in Europe. But perhaps the most intriguing excavation is the large fortress bath-house, where the Romans would swim, enjoy games and sports, and enjoy the hot and cold baths. The excavations are administered by Cadw-Welsh Historic Monuments. Caerleon Roman Fortress Baths are open summer daily 9.30–6.30, winter Monday–Saturday 9.30–4, Sunday 2–4. Telephone: (01633) 422518.

Many of the finds unearthed at Caerleon are displayed at the town's Roman Legionary Museum. Open summer Monday–Saturday 10–6, Sunday 2–6, winter Monday–Saturday 10–4.30, Sunday 2–4.30. Telephone: (01633) 423134.

Usk is famous for its floral displays

In 1½ miles by White Castle Cottage, take the short detour left off this minor road for White Castle. After visiting this key border stronghold, proceed northwards on the minor road, turning left on to the B4521 for Abergavenny.

Within a few miles, on your right, you will pass the Walnut Tree Inn. Although its appearance is nothing out of the ordinary, the Walnut Tree is no average country pub. Run for many years by Franco and Ann Taruschio, it is one of the very best restaurants in Wales. If it is lunchtime, and you are in the mood for a special treat, stop off here.

On the approach to Abergavenny where the B4521 meets the A465 , stay on the 'B' road for the town centre (do not turn on to the A465 southwards; it bypasses the town). In the town, follow the signs for the A40 (eastbound). At the large roundabout on the southern outskirts, take the B4598 for Usk, an attractive little town noted for its floral displays.

On the way into Usk, the road runs beside the river of the same name. The Usk, like the Wye, is a prized fishing river, renowned for its salmon and trout.

In Usk, turn right where the B4598 meets the A472 (by the Three Salmons Hotel) , and immediately left on to the minor road southwards after crossing the river. If you have the time, it is worth stopping off here, perhaps to wander through Usk's spacious town square, lined with handsome buildings, or to visit the Gwent Rural Life Museum which covers local life from Victorian times to World War II. Usk, like other border settlements, also boasts a castle dating from Norman times, though in this case it is in private ownership and has been partially converted into a house.

From Usk, follow the minor road south along the Usk Valley through Llangybi to Caerleon. Caerleon does not receive the attention it deserves. One of the Romans' main bases in Britain, it has a wealth of remains – some exceedingly well preserved –including an amphitheatre and excavated bath-house complex. Allow at least a few hours to see it all.

Leave Caerleon by the B4236. Just over 1 mile after crossing the river, turn left on to the A48 , staying on this road at the next major roundabout under the M4.

Stay on the A48, in the direction of Chepstow. In a few miles, Penhow Castle comes into view. With its restored Norman bedchamber and fifteenth-century Great Hall, the fortified manor house of Penhow claims to be Wales's oldest lived-in castle. There is no doubting the authenticity of the Roman remains at Caerwent, a little further along the A48. It was known to the Romans as *Venta Silurum*, the 'town of the Silures' (a local tribe they had conquered). Caerwent still has stretches of perimeter wall – some of which stand to a height of 17 feet (5 m) – dating back 2,000 years to the time when it was an important Roman 'new town'.

Shortly, the A48 brings you back to Chepstow. ∎

Chepstow Castle, on its bluff overlooking the River Wye

CARDIFF AND THE EASTERN VALLEYS

46 MILES – 2 ½ HOURS
START AND FINISH AT CARDIFF CITY CENTRE

The frenetic, fascinating industrial history of South Wales is a major theme all the way along this route. Cardiff grew up as a seaport serving the industrial valleys, its opulent architecture a testament to the fortunes created in the nineteenth century. There is further evidence of great industrial wealth at Tredegar House, Newport. As industry declined, the valleys became green again – as you will see at places like Cwmcarn, where a scenic drive leads up through the trees. Even more historic interest is added at the close of the tour, which takes in two castles, medieval Caerphilly and fairytale Castell Coch.

Shopping arcade, Cardiff

Cardiff's impressive neoclassical Civic Centre of white-stoned buildings, which includes the domed City Hall and neighbouring National Museum and Gallery, makes a convenient starting point for this tour (Cardiff is not the easiest city when it comes to parking; the best concentration of long-term car parks is within a short distance of the Civic Centre just to the north of the main shopping streets).

Leave Cardiff along Newport Road (signposted Newport and M4) A. Newport Road is lined with large garages and out-of-town stores. **Bear left** along the slip road to the A48 after the main Ford (Evans Halshaw) dealership (on your left). The A48 subsequently joins the A48 (M) and the M4.

Stay on the M4 until the outskirts of Newport. **Leave the motorway at junction 28 B for a short detour to Tredegar House Country Park (the entrance is signposted from the motorway).**

Although within a stone's throw of a major road intersection, this outstanding red-bricked mansion, set in its own grounds just west of Newport's city centre, is a picture of peace and tranquillity.

After visiting Tredegar House return to the M4 eastbound for a short distance, leaving at junction 27 on the B4591 north-westwards through High Cross towards Risca, taking the short detour to the right to Fourteen Locks Canal Centre (signposted) just after High Cross.

Fourteen Locks is a monument to the ambition and indomitable spirit of the engineers of the Canal Age. Faced with the problem of raising the Monmouthshire and Brecon Canal 168 feet (51 m) up a hillside in a distance of only half a mile, they proceeded to cut a huge staircase of lock chambers – 14 in all – into the hill. You can walk down beside the locks by following a path from the car park, where there is a small canal exhibition centre.

Tredegar House, on the outskirts of Newport

From Fourteen Locks, continue north-westwards on the B4591. As you travel, you will notice a gradual but distinct change in the topography and the character of the towns. The flattish plain of the Severn Estuary gives way to narrowing, steep-sided valleys. In these confined spaces, urban development is concentrated along the valley floors in a linear pattern, one town blending into the next.

On leaving Risca, go straight on at the junction, following the sign to Newbridge and Abertillery (A467). You are still on the B4591, which brings you to Crosskeys.

The route follows the valley of the River Ebbw, which originates near the old steelmaking town of Ebbw Vale. This part of South Wales still has an unmistakeable industrial atmosphere, even though the coalmines and heavy industry which once sustained it have long since departed.

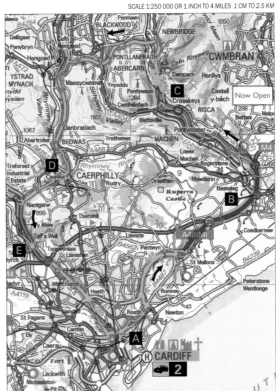

• PLACES OF INTEREST •

Cardiff

Cardiff grew up in the nineteenth century as a coal-exporting port. The tremendous wealth created during those hectic days was used to good effect – the immensely rich Bute family, owners of Cardiff docks, built a fabulous Victorian mansion on the site of Cardiff's medieval castle, and also bequeathed large areas of parkland which became the basis of Cardiff's splendid Civic Centre.

Cardiff, which was declared the Welsh capital in 1955, is really a city of two parts. With the decline of the docks earlier in the twentieth century, Cardiff's focal point moved northwards. The modern heart of Cardiff lies around its castle and Civic Centre, though the balance is beginning to change again with the wholesale redevelopment of the Cardiff Bay waterfront (see Tour 3 for details).

The neoclassical grace of Cardiff's white-stoned Civic Centre comes as a surprise to those brought up on the old 'Tiger Bay' image of the city. This collection of government and civic buildings had been rated along with Washington DC and New Delhi as one of the world's most elegant examples of civic architecture. Fronting the Civic Centre is the great dome of the City Hall, topped by a Welsh dragon. It is worth venturing in to see the 'Heroes of Wales' statues in the Marble Hall.

Next door is the National Museum and Gallery, a treasure chest of anything and everything to do with Wales and Welsh life – and more besides, for the museum also has a world-famous collection of French Impressionist paintings, including priceless works by Monet, Renoir and Van Gogh. One of the museum's highlights is the 'Evolution of Wales' gallery, an imaginative trip through time involving the latest display techniques. Open Tuesday–Sunday 10–5. Telephone: (01222) 397951.

Cardiff Castle is a must. The Romans built a fort here, the Normans added a castle to the site, and the Marquess of Bute lavished much of his wealth on creating a Victorian fantasy palace. All three periods are represented at this large city-centre site, though the abiding memory is of the stunning sequence of rooms, dripping with decorative embellishment and romantic allusion, which so accurately reflect the spirit of Victorian times. Open: please telephone for times, together with details of guided tour. Telephone: (01222) 822083.

Close to the castle is an attractive shopping centre, noted for its wealth of Victorian and Edwardian canopied arcades which weave in amongst more modern developments. Also close by – its position unusually central for a major sport stadium – is Cardiff Arms Park, the spiritual home of rugby for fans the world over.

Tredegar House and Country Park, Newport

Located on the outskirts of Newport, Tredegar House was home for at least five centuries to one of the great Welsh families, the Morgans of Tredegar. The elegant red-bricked mansion owes much of its grandeur to the fortunes that were made by the family at Newport's booming nineteenth-century docklands. Dating from the seventeenth century and widely regarded as one of the most magnificent Charles II houses in the whole of Britain, Tredegar House offers a fascinating insight into the 'upstairs, downstairs' life of a gentry family, with tours available that take in the servants' quarters as well as the glittering interiors.

Attractions in the surrounding park include a boating lake, adventure playground, carriage rides, craft workshops, Edwardian sunken garden, a series of walled gardens and restored orangery garden. Open Easter–September, Wednesday–Sunday 11.30–4, and also weekends in October. Telephone: (01633) 815880.

Caerphilly Castle

The strategic importance of this outstanding castle is best appreciated from the lofty vantage point of Caerphilly Mountain on the northern outkirts of Cardiff. Caerphilly is one of the greatest castles of the medieval western world, occupying a 30-acre (12-hectare) site which is equalled in size among British castles only by Dover and Windsor.

The castle's massive gatehouses, water defences and concentric walls meant that it was virtually impregnable against contemporary siege methods. Built by 'Red Gilbert' de Clare to defend his territory against Welsh prince Llywelyn the Last, this massive engineering feat was achieved in just two decades, most of the work being carried out between 1268 and 1271. The only weakness here is the castle's famous 'leaning tower' which teeters 10 degrees from the vertical, out-leaning even the Tower of Pisa. Open summer daily 9.30–6.30, winter Monday–Saturday 9.30–4, Sunday 11–4. Telephone: (01222) 883143.

Castell Coch, Tongwynlais

Peeping through the trees, Castell Coch is an enchanting castle which combines Victorian fantasy and timeless fairytale. Created by the fabulously wealth Marquess of Bute and architect William Burges, it was intended as a country retreat and companion piece to the marquess's main home at Cardiff Castle. Like its big brother, Castell Coch is a decorative extravaganza, inspired by an eclectic range of visual influences which embrace everything from Aesop's fables to Greek mythology. As a final flourish, this extraordinary invention was equipped with a fully operational portcullis and drawbridge. Open summer daily 9.30–6.30, winter Monday–Saturday 9.30–4, Sunday 11–4. Telephone: (01222) 810101.

Stop off for a mountain walk on the Cwmcarn Forest Scenic Drive

At the traffic lights on the northern end of Crosskeys go straight on, signposted Cwmcarn Forest Scenic Drive. This road shortly joins the A467, where you turn right **C**. In a short distance, take the detour right off the A467 for the Forest Drive, again signposted.

Despite the industrial past, the valleys have an unexpected and dramatic beauty. Land reclamation and environmental improvement schemes have removed old scars, conifer forests clothe the hillsides, and the mountaintops – which never saw any industrial exploitation – possess a wild natural beauty. These features are nowhere better demonstrated than at Cwmcarn.

After following the Forest Drive, return to the A467 northwards to Newbridge. From the large roundabout at the approach to Newbridge,

Formidable stone and water defences protect Caerphilly Castle

drive westwards along the **A472 to Ystrad Mynach.**

Just over halfway along the road from Newbridge to Ystrad Mynach you can take a short detour south along the A4048 at Gelligroes (the second roundabout along the dual-carriageway) for the Old Mill. This fully operational seventeenth-century stone-built watermill on the River Sirhowy, originally engaged in flour grinding, has interpretive displays. An adjacent workshop specialising in handmade candles is also open to visitors.

On the approach to Ystrad Mynach, look out on your right for the Hengoed Viaduct (sometimes called the Maes-y-Cymmer Viaduct). This 15-arched stone-built viaduct, designed in 1857 to carry the Newport, Abergavenny and Hereford Railway across the valley, is an outstanding industrial monument. **At Ystrad Mynach, take the A469 southwards down the Rhymney Valley to Caerphilly.** There is a convenient car park in the middle of Caerphilly next to the tourist information centre and just a short walk from the town's

extraordinary medieval castle, judged by military historians to be one of the finest in Europe.

Leave Caerphilly westbound along the B4600 D , the road just north of the castle. After just over a mile, this road joins the A468, which drops down the hillside at Nantgarw to the A470 southwards to Cardiff. Nantgarw was once famous for its

fine porcelain. The industry was founded in 1813 by William Billingsley, one of Royal Worcester's most eminent artists, and continued to operate until 1920. At the Nantgarw China Works visitor centre, the kilns and other remains of the pottery are arranged in a series of terraces above the old village and alongside the course of the Glamorganshire Canal.

The dual-carriageway A470 follows the River Taff along another historic vale – possibly the most significant valley of them all. It was along the Taff Valley that coal was transported to the booming docklands in Cardiff, which led to the former coastal village becoming the capital city of Wales.

The valley narrows into a gorge just beyond Taff's Well, guarded by a castle (Cadw-Welsh Historic Monuments) straight out of Walt Disney perched on the precipitous wooded eastern slope. **To visit the castle leave the A470 at Tongwynlais for Castell Coch (signposted) E .**

The road through Tongwynlais rejoins the A470 at the large intersection under the M4. Rejoin the A470 here for the centre of Cardiff. ■

Fairytale Castell Coch, Tongwynlais

CARDIFF, THE VALE OF GLAMORGAN AND THE GLAMORGAN HERITAGE COAST

48 MILES – 2 ½ HOURS
START AND FINISH AT CARDIFF

Pleasant countryside and coastline are features of this tour, together with glimpses into Wales's past and future. The Museum of Welsh Life at St Fagans, one of Britain's first and finest open-air museums, looks at Wales through the ages. In contrast, the Cardiff of tomorrow is taking shape along the redeveloping waterfront. Elsewhere, the tour takes you to pretty villages and historic sites in the green farmlands of the Vale of Glamorgan, which is fringed by a spectacular coast.

Llandaff's High Street, the pretty little main thoroughfare, is lined with shops and pubs. It leads to a delightful Green and the well-kept ruins of a medieval Bishop's Palace. The cathedral itself lies in a steep, grassy hollow beneath the Green, alongside the River Taff.

After visiting the cathedral, retrace your route back to the major road junction on the southern approach to Llandaff, turning right here at the traffic lights signposted Port Talbot A48. In just over ½ mile, turn right at the traffic lights signposted Welsh Folk Museum, a road which takes you through the Fairwater district of the city. Stay on this road, which in less than 2 miles brings you to St Fagans, home of the Museum of Welsh Life (Welsh Folk Museum).

It is surprising how abruptly the urban fringes of Cardiff give way to countryside. Although less than a mile from the sprawl of Fairwater, St Fagans has all the attributes of a picturesque country village.

At the T-junction in the village, turn left down the hill. The entrance to the Museum of Welsh Life is on your right at the bottom of the hill before the river. The museum covers a lot of ground, both in size and content. Give yourself a few hours here, more if you can spare the time.

Leave the centre of Cardiff by Cathedral Road A (just west of the city-centre castle). **Drive along this road for 1 mile, turning right at the** traffic lights on the hill. At the next two sets of lights continue straight on for the pleasant 'village' suburb of Llandaff.

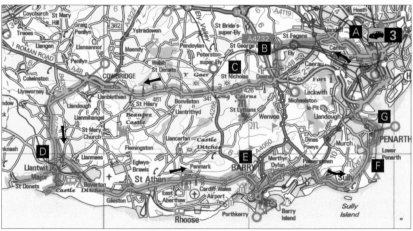

SCALE 1:250 000 OR 1 INCH TO 4 MILES *1 CM TO 2.5 KM*

Inside Llandaff Cathedral, Cardiff

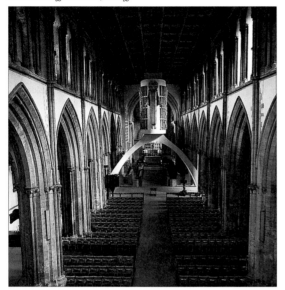

roofs are still very much in evidence. The Vale, a well-drained fertile lowland area, stretches all the way westwards to Bridgend. Supporting a prosperous mixed agriculture of crops and cattle, it is sometimes known as the 'Garden of Wales'.

At St Nicholas, take a detour left █ along the minor road for Tinkinswood Burial Chamber (Cadw-Welsh Historic Monuments) and Dyffryn Gardens. Tinkinswood, standing in fields shortly on your right, is an outstanding prehistoric site. Its giant capstone, weighing 40 tons and measuring 24 feet (7 m), sits on top of a large burial chamber built by neolithic settlers around 3,500 years ago. The bones of at least 50 people and items of pottery were found here when the tomb was excavated in the early twentieth century. A little further along the minor road is the entrance to Dyffryn Gardens (see Places of Interest).

From St Nicholas, drive westwards along the A48,

Leave St Fagans by the minor road █ to the south by the level crossing over the railway line, which leads to the A48. Turn right here (by the Wyndham Garage), and within a very short distance follow the signs for Dyffryn Gardens and the A48 westbound at the major intersection at Culverhouse Cross.

This marks the start of the Vale of Glamorgan, a swathe of rich, green farming country dotted with pretty villages where thatched

---

• PLACES OF INTEREST •

Llandaff Cathedral
The cathedral stands on a site which has witnessed religious worship since the sixth century. The present cathedral, its soaring twin towers peeping out of a steep hollow, is medieval in origin. Severely damaged by a German landmine in 1941, it was subsequently restored to its former glory, with two striking differences – the addition of the Welch Regiment Chapel and, more controversially, the uncompromisingly modernistic statue *Christ in Majesty* by Sir Jacob Epstein, which dominates the interior.

Museum of Welsh Life, St Fagans
If you cannot fit a full tour of Wales into your travel plans, then this museum is the next best thing. Buildings from all over Wales

representing different periods and preoccupations have been brought to St Fagans to be re-erected, stone-by-stone, timber-by-timber in beautiful parklands. There are farmhouses, a chapel, baker, village store, toll-house, cockpit, school, rural workshops, a row of workers' cottages and much else besides, all of which paint an authentic picture of Wales in bygone times. In addition to the open-air exhibits there is a conventional, purpose-built museum block. A handsome Elizabethan mansion, around which the museum has grown up,

is also on site. Open July–September, daily 10–6, October–June, daily 10–5. Telephone: (01222) 569441.

Dyffryn Gardens, near St Nicholas
Dyffryn is one of the finest and largest landscaped gardens in Wales. Its 70 acres (28 hectares) are ranged around Dyffryn House, a grand late nineteenth-century mansion now used as a conference centre. The gardens display a variety of features, from vast lawns to formal gardens, theme gardens to plant houses. There are lots of individual rare and exotic plants and trees, and plants from all over the world are grown in the Temperate House. Other highlights include an arboretum, rose garden and pool garden, Please telephone for opening times. Telephone: (01222) 593328.

leaving on the A4222 at the eastern approach of Cowbridge for the town centre. The handsome 'Capital of the Vale', Cowbridge is an affluent town with an excellent range of shops, pubs and places to eat – and all the better for being bypassed by the A48, which used to sweep through the main street. It was established as a market town by the Normans, and the medieval street pattern is still evident, together with parts of the original town walls and south gateway.

Leave Cowbridge by the main street, the A4222 westwards, shortly turning left on to the B4270 for Llantwit Major. This characterful town of narrow streets and old buildings, clustered around its ancient church, convincingly retains a look of bygone times. Its massive, cathedral-like church has a special religious status as the site of the first Christian college in Britain. It is named after St Illtyd, the fifth-century leader of a monastic and educational community where St David, Wales's patron saint, was reputedly taught. St Illtyd's Church is a grand affair – in effect, two buildings in one – made up of adjacent churches from the early twelfth and late thirteenth centuries. It contains a notable collection of Celtic crosses and inscribed stones.

Dyffryn Gardens

There are two short detours at Llantwit Major D – the first to St Donat's, following the minor road from the centre of the town 2 miles to the west, and the second to the little beach at Col-huw, following the minor road south from the town centre for a mile.

Col-huw is the first sight of the sea on this tour. The little beach stands on the Glamorgan Heritage Coast, a 14-mile stretch designated as one of three pilot 'Heritage Coasts' in the early 1970s. This spectacular, but often inaccessible coastline runs from Porthcawl in the west to Aberthaw in the east and is made up of cliffs, rocks, wave-cut platforms and secluded bays.

From Llantwit Major, take the B4265 eastwards for Barry. This road skirts St Athan, location of a large RAF base, and joins the A4226 for Barry at the roundabout by

• *PLACES OF INTEREST* •

St Donat's
The castle here has surprising connections with the fabulous San Simeon Castle on the Californian coast. Both were owned by the American newspaper tycoon William Randolph Hearst. The castle, dating from the fourteenth to sixteenth centuries, was restored in appropriate baronial style by Hearst in the 1930s. In 1962 it became the home of Atlantic College, the world's first international college. It is open for guided tours in summer. Telephone: (01446) 792271. St Donat's Arts Centre is an art gallery and concert venue in a converted fourteenth-century tithe barn.

Cosmeston Lakes Country Park
The two lakes here provide a focal point for a 200-acre (81-hectare) country park with a wide range of amenities. It is difficult to believe that this beautifully landscaped area was once a limestone quarry and refuse tip. The lakesides and their surrounding meadows and woodland can be explored by nature trails, there are bridleways for horse riders, and the eastern lake is used for a variety of watersports, including sailing and windsurfing. Within the park there are several nature conservation areas. Other amenities include an adventure playground, picnic areas and an extremely informative visitor centre. Park open dawn to dusk. Visitor centre open summer daily 10–6, winter daily 10–5. Telephone: (01222) 701678.

Cardiff Bay
Cardiff intends to reunite with its maritime past by the twenty-first century. The old docklands are being transformed by the ambitious Cardiff Bay development. The strange silver tube on the waterfront, which everyone compares to a UFO, houses the Cardiff Bay Visitor Centre, containing models and details of the changing waterfront.

Wisely, some of the history is being preserved. The nearby Norwegian Church, built for visiting seamen, is now a cultural centre and café (author Roald Dahl was baptised here). Exhibits at the Welsh Industrial and Maritime Museum recall Cardiff's boom years. And the self-important Victorian buildings around Mount Stuart Square are reminders of Cardiff's stature as one of the world's great coal-exporting ports. On a more modern note, the waterfront is also home to Techniquest, an entertaining and educational science discovery centre.

Wales International Airport. At the roundabout **E** on the northern outskirts of Barry, take the B4266 for the town, which joins the A4055 for Barry Island. Barry is a strange mixture of town, docks and traditional 'fun-of-the-fair' seaside resort. The docks were founded by nineteenth-century coal owner David Davies to export the coal which flowed from the Rhondda and neighbouring valleys. Barry Island can also look to the valleys for its roots, for it grew up as a resort popular with the mining communities. The 'Island' is in fact a promontory, dominated by a large pleasure park and the extensive sands of Whitmore Bay. Barry's quieter side is to be found to the west at Cold Knap, where gardens and a boating lake back a long pebble beach which leads to Porthkerry Country Park.

Leave Barry by the A4055, turning on to the B4267 for Sully and Penarth. The entrance to Cosmeston Lakes Country Park and Medieval Village is on your left between Sully and Penarth.

After visiting the Cosmeston Lakes Country Park, return to the B4267, turning left. In ½ mile on the approach to Penarth, turn right off the B4267 signposted Town Centre and Sea Front F. Continue on this suburban road for just over ¼ mile, turning right on to Raisdale Road at the crossroads (unsignposted) which brings you shortly to the seafront.

Penarth began life as a Victorian seaside resort, though nowadays it has almost become a suburb of Cardiff. Nevertheless, traditional touches remain – the pretty seafront Alexandra Park, the ornate pier, the promenade and clifftop walks. The town's Turner House Gallery stages varied and changing exhibitions of paintings and *objets d'art*. Around the headland, Penarth is

equipping itself for a new leisure market at its modern marina.

From Penarth seafront, leave in the direction of Cardiff. At the roundabout at the northern end of the town, take the detour for Penarth Marina (signposted) G.

After visiting the marina, return to the roundabout for Cardiff, shortly taking the A4055 over the bridge at the next roundabout which brings you to the intersection with the A4160 (on this section of dual-carriageway road from Penarth to the new Cardiff Bay waterfront development, keep following the signs to the Docks, Cardiff Bay and the Inner Harbour).

The road travels through the Queen's Gate tunnel before reaching the waterfront.

You will see much evidence of change along the old waterfront, where in the early twentieth century the docks exported record amounts of coal. The rejuvenation of Cardiff Bay is one of Europe's most exciting

Llantwit Major

maritime redevelopments. Millions of pounds are being spent to create a freshwater lake and new 8-mile waterfront where the Cardiff of the twenty-first century will live, work and play. The development is already taking shape: for the best overview, go first to the Cardiff Bay Visitor Centre, then take a stroll along the new seafront walkway past the flamboyant Pierhead Building.

After visiting the waterfront, return to the city centre. ■

Pier and seafront gardens at Penarth

ABERGAVENNY AND THE BLACK MOUNTAINS

47 MILES – 2 ½ HOURS
START AND FINISH AT ABERGAVENNY

This tour takes in contrasting scenery and historic sites. It ventures through the remote Black Mountains on the eastern flank of the Brecon Beacons National Park, crossing them by a narrow, spectacular road. There are also gentle stretches of route alongside the Wye and Usk rivers. Places to visit include secluded religious settlements and castles. Bibliophiles should bring their cheque books: the tour's halfway point is Hay-on-Wye, world famous for its many bookshops.

Abergavenny is a bustling country town with a cosmopolitan air. There is a large car park on the main Abergavenny to Brecon road through the town, opposite the entrance to the pedestrianised shopping precinct. The only difficult day for parking is Tuesday, when Abergavenny is completely taken over by a large livestock mart and open-air traders' market. It is worth struggling through the crowds, for the town has a lively atmosphere on market day – and you may even pick up a bargain or two.

From Abergavenny town centre, follow the A40 southwards (in the direction of the railway station, Raglan and Monmouth). At the large roundabout on the southern outskirts of the town take the A465 northwards towards Hereford.

The road follows the broad Gavenny Valley, flanked by hills. Within a mile or so you will pass an isolated mountain on your right.

· PLACES OF INTEREST ·

Abergavenny
This attractive town stands beside the River Usk at the south-eastern gateway to the Brecon Beacons National Park. Ruined Abergavenny Castle, in green fields above the river, was the scene of an infamous episode in Welsh history. During the Christmas of 1176, the Norman lord William be Breos invited a group of Welsh noblemen to the castle to hear a supposed royal proclamation, only to massacre them within the castle walls. A renovated part of the castle contains a museum whose exhibits include a Welsh farmhouse kitchen and frequently changing displays. Museum open March–October, Monday–Saturday 11–1, 2–5, November–February Monday–Saturday 11–1, 2–4. Telephone: (01873) 854282.

Abergavenny's other museum, dedicated to Childhood and the Home, is housed in a former chapel. Within are all kinds of childhood memorabilia – dolls, teddy bears, toys and games – together with period room settings. Open summer Monday–Saturday 10–5, Sunday 1–5. Please telephone for winter openings. Telephone: (01873) 850063.

The town's long main street and modern precinct are popular shopping venues, and – in addition to the main market on Tuesday – there are regular Saturday covered markets in the Victorian Town Hall. Close to the town centre are the lovely Linda Vista Gardens and the large Bailey Park, with many leisure facilities.

Llanthony Priory
According to the medieval traveller and chronicler Giraldus Cambrensis, Gerald of Wales, no place was more 'truly calculated for religion' than Llanthony. Today, visitors to this remote spot, with its ruined priory and scattering of farms, can still experience the sense of sanctity which Giraldus described. Religious men in search of solitude founded a monastery here in the twelfth century. The shell of their red-stoned ruin stands in fields beneath a mountain ridge which markes the border between Wales and England.

In the nineteenth century, poet Walter Savage Landor acquired the property with grand plans to install himself as a model country gentleman. This miscast lord of the manor left under a cloud in 1813, never to return. The priory's former magnificence can be glimpsed in the row of pointed arches which survive almost intact. Unusually, there is a small inn and hotel built into part of the priory where the abbot would once have lived. Free access.

This is Ysgyryd Fawr, known locally as The Skirrid, a strangely shaped mountain rising to 1,595 feet (486 m). According to legend, the unusual chasm at the summit was caused by God at the Crucifixion of Christ. Its boulder-strewn summit subsequently became a place of pilgrimage, and there are faint remains of a chapel dedicated to St Michael.

Turn left off the A465 at Llanvihangel Crucorney A. Turn left again after the Skirrid Inn, which claims to be one of the oldest pubs in Wales, in the middle of the village.

Follow the road north through the remote Vale of Ewyas alongside the River Honddu. You are now entering the Black Mountains, a highland fastness of bare-topped peaks which fills the Wales–England border. This mountain range, part of the Brecon Beacons National Park, is popular with walkers and pony trekking enthusiasts (you will see signs for trekking centres along the road).

Within a mile or so of Llanvihangel Crucorney you can take a short detour to Cwmyoy on the opposite side of the valley to visit the incredible Church of St Martin. It is a miracle that this topsy-turvy church still stands, for subsidence has played havoc with its foundations. Floors and walls tilt at drunken angles, and the precarious tower is supported by buttresses.

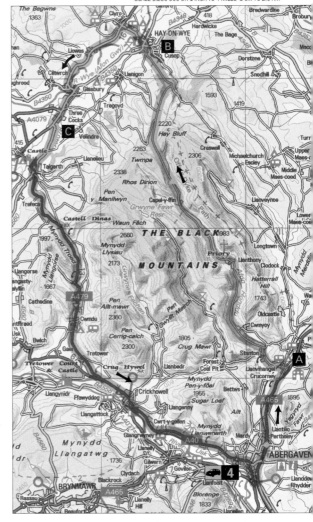

The minor road up the valley as far as the hamlet of Llanthony is wide. Beyond, it narrows considerably – to the point that it may be unwise to

follow this route on peak weekends in summer, unless you enjoy reversing or pulling in to let oncoming cars through. At other times, traffic is light, although special care should be taken in the narrow sections.

Llanthony itself is a captivating spot locked away in the mountains and consisting of no more than a few houses, a pub and priory ruins (Cadw-Welsh Historic Monuments). From the car park beside the priory, a footpath climbs up to the summit of the ridge (the Wales/England border) which is traversed by the long-distance Offa's Dyke Path. The views from this lofty spot, overlooking the Welsh mountains

Remote Llanthony Priory, hidden deep in the mountains

27

Bookshops, bookshops everywhere at Hay-on-Wye

to the west and Golden Valley and the flat Herefordshire plains to the east, are breathtaking.

From Llanthony, follow the road northward to Capel-y-ffin. There is a tiny eighteenth-century roadside chapel here with the inscription 'I will lift up mine eyes unto the hills from whence cometh my help' on one of its windows. This remote valley seems to inspire religious sentiments, for on the hillside to the left stand the privately owned ruins of Llanthony Abbey, a short-lived monastery originally founded by the enigmatic Father Ignatius (1837–1908), which later became the home of artist Eric Gill.

The medieval keep at Tretower

The road now climbs steeply up the Gospel Pass. From the 1,778-foot (542 m) summit there are vast views northwards across farmland and mountain. This spectacular mountain road, the highest in South Wales, tracks across open moorland between Hay Bluff (2,220 feet/677 m) and Lord Hereford's Knob (2,263 feet/ 690 m), the northernmost summits of the Black Mountains. The west-facing ridges are a favourite spot for hang gliders, while walkers have a choice of challenging mountain paths to the west and east.

From these airy wildernesses, the road descends just as abruptly into the civilised calm of Hay-on-Wye, the borderland 'town of books'. There is a large car park at Hay next to the Tourist Information Centre and complex of craft shops.

Leave Hay-on-Wye by turning left ▣ over the bridge across the river for Clyro (the B4351). Clyro was the home of Francis Kilvert, the nineteenth-century curate who wrote the immensely popular *Kilvert's Diaries* which describes the places and people of the border country. He lived in Ash Brook House while serving as the local curate; there is a commemorative stone to him in the village church.

From Clyro, take the A438 to Glasbury. Fans of Kilvert will want to stop off at Llowes, between Clyro and Glasbury, where the diarist is again remembered, this time by a commemorative sundial in the churchyard. Inside the church there is a Celtic cross dating back to AD600. The minor road to the right about a mile after Llowes and ½ mile before Glasbury leads up the hill to a small chapel of great historic significance. Maesyronnen Chapel, founded around 1696, was one of the earliest places of worship for Nonconformism, a religious

Hay-on-Wye

Thirty years ago you could have driven through Hay and thought little of the place. Nowadays, Hay is the world-famous 'town of books', a role model to any enterprising community wanting to put itself on the map. Following the opening of the first bookshop came a flood of others. Between them all, Hay's 20 or 30 bookshops now cover everything from cheap second-hand novels to expensive antiquarian tomes, discounted new books to rare specialist titles. Hay is a book-lover's paradise – it is easy to spend an entire day here browsing through the bookshops which dominate this little border town. There are even bookshops in the old cinema and fire station!

Along with books have come other shops. Hay is also a good place for antiques, prints and crafts. The town is not without its interesting architectural features. In the centre is the old Butter Market dating from 1833, while close by, on a hill overlooking the main street, stands Hay Castle, a partly ruined seventeenth-century mansion on the site of the town's Norman stronghold. Appropriately enough, Hay is now

the location for a well-regarded Festival of Literature in early summer, which attracts major international celebrities.

Tretower Court and Castle

Tretower is a two-in-one historic site which illustrates how the military imperatives of the earlier medieval period were eventually replaced by more domestic considerations in later, more peaceful times. Firstly there is Tretower's circular stone keep, plainly military in design, put up in the thirteenth century on the site of an earlier stronghold. It stands close to Tretower's great glory, its splendid court, which dates from the more settled fourteenth century when the castle's residents felt secure enough to move to a new, more comfortable home.

As it stands today, Tretower Court is mainly fifteenth century, and contains superb examples of late-medieval craftsmanship in stone and wood. Interestingly, it is similar in plan to the colleges of Oxford and Cambridge. Open summer daily 9.30–6.30, winter Monday–Saturday 9.30–4, Sunday 2–4. Telephone: (01874) 730279.

movement which subsequently spread throughout Wales. Its authentic period atmosphere is remarkable, not least due to its original eighteenth- and

nineteenth-century furnishings.

Continue along the A438, crossing the River Wye at Glasbury, and drive through Three Cocks. After Three

Cocks, turn left off the A438 on to the A4078 for Talgarth. From Talgarth, take the A479 south for Abergavenny, which climbs over the mountains. At the summit 3 miles from Talgarth, you can take a short detour for a walk to the Iron Age hillfort of Castell Dinas. Turn left just after the telephone box and within ¼ mile park near the end of the surfaced road. Follow the unmade road past the farm and up the hill to park. Walk through the field at the top to the summit of Castell Dinas, in a commanding location surveying the pass.

The A479 leads down the valley to Tretower, a village noted for its manor house and castle (Cadw-Welsh Historic Monuments). Just beyond Tretower, the A479 joins the A40. Turn left here for Crickhowell.

It is worth stopping off at the attractive little town of Crickhowell. The Bear Hotel in the centre is a famous hostelry which displays mementoes of its past as a coaching inn. There is a pleasant riverside walk along the Usk from the town's many-arched bridge, which dates from the sixteenth century. In parklands behind the main street are the ruins of a Norman castle.

From Crickhowell, return to Abergavenny. ■

Crickhowell's old bridge spans the beautiful Usk Valley

MERTHYR TYDFIL AND
THE NORTHERN VALLEYS

57 MILES – 3 HOURS
START AND FINISH AT MERTHYR TYDFIL

Although this tour concentrates on South Wales's industrial heritage, there are a few surprising interludes. The dividing line between industrial and rural South Wales is very sharply drawn, as you will see when on the route into the Brecon Beacons National Park. The valleys themselves also have their surprises. At Llancaiach Fawr, for example, there is an atmospheric Tudor manor house, while the route across the windy tops of the valleys north from Gelligaer is an exhilarating away-from-it-all experience.

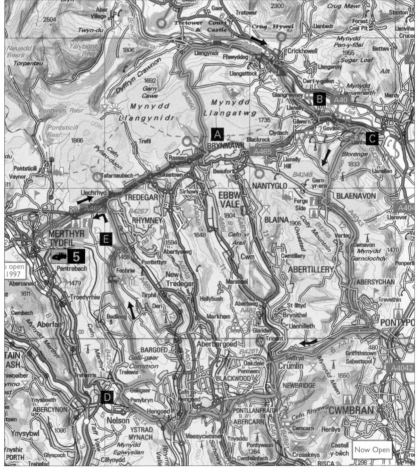

SCALE 1:250 000 OR 1 INCH TO 4 MILES *1 CM TO 2.5 KM*

From the centre of Merthyr take the A4102 north-eastwards towards Abergavenny. This road climbs up through Dowlais (the old iron- and steel-making district of Merthyr), in 2 miles joining the A465 'Heads of the Valleys' road at the roundabout beside the Asda superstore. Take the A465 in the direction of Abergavenny.

The three-lane 'Heads of the Valleys' road is a major east-west communications artery. It runs along the northern fringes of the South Wales valleys, acting almost as a boundary between industrial and rural Wales. The road more or less runs along a line where the coal-bearing rocks of the south meet the Old Red Sandstones of the Brecon Beacons. These geological differences have had a profound effect on the scenery and social development of South Wales. To your right you will see the towns and villages which grew up around ironworks and coalmines in the eighteenth and nineteenth centuries. Untouched moorlands, the beginnings of the Brecon Beacons National Park, stretch away as far as the eye can see to the north of the road.

The largest town directly accessible off the 'Heads of the Valleys' is Ebbw Vale, once a major producer of steel. Much of the old steelworks site south of the town was transformed in the early 1990s in preparation for the Garden Festival of 1992. Millions of pounds were spent on the wholesale remodelling of derelict industrial land, leaving the town with an attractive Festival Park which retains many features of the event. **If you are intrigued to see the results of Britain's last Garden Festival, take the A4046 into Ebbw Vale and follow the main road through the town to the Festival Park.**

Back on the 'Heads of the Valleys', turn left off the A465 on to the B4560, signposted Llangynidr .

• PLACES OF INTEREST •

Merthyr Tydfil

In its industrial heyday, Merthyr Tydfil was the 'iron and steel capital' of the world. Its work produced metal used as far away as South America in the building of the railways there. There is no one site which sums up the enormity of Merthyr's former role. Instead, the town has a scattering of places which, taken together, illustrate Merthyr's industrial and cultural achievements. The attractively restored Ynysfach Engine House near the town centre has displays on the iron and steel industry and a 'Story of Iron' audio-visual. Close by is Joseph Parry's Cottage, a tiny house-cum-museum dedicated to Merthyr's most famous nineteenth-century composer.

The most impressive place of all is Cyfarthfa Castle, standing in its own grounds north of the town centre. This mock castle, built in 1824, has an imperious quality – which was no doubt the intention of its owners, the all-powerful Crawshay ironmasters. Within the castle, there is a superb museum covering everything from art to industrial heritage. South Wales's debt to the Italian immigrants who opened cafés in the industrial valleys is remembered at the museum's enchanting Café Bardi, where you can enjoy a cup of cappuccino. The castle stands in a 160-acre (65-hectare) park with a lake, woodland walk and leisure facilities. Museum open April–September, Monday–Friday 10–6, weekends 12–6. October–March, Monday–Friday 10–5, weekends 12–5. Telephone: (01685) 723112.

Although perceived as an industrial town, Methyr is on the doorstep of the Brecon Beacons National Park. The narrow-gauge Brecon Mountain Railway runs from a station at Pant at the northern edge of Merthyr on a scenic route to a lakeside halt in the foothills of the Brecons. Open all year. Telephone: (01685) 722988.

Monmouthshire and Brecon Canal

This inland waterway runs through some of the loveliest scenery in the Brecon Beacons National Park. Dating from the end of the eighteenth century, it was built to connect Brecon with Newport and the Severn Estuary. It carried limestone and coal from nearby quarries and mines, together with other goods such as wool, timber and food. Its productive years were short, for railways soon came along and the canal fell into disuse. Following restoration, it was reopened in 1970 between Brecon and Pontypool, a distance of 33 miles. The waterway, the only British canal to run entirely within a national park, now has a new lease of life thanks to the canal cruisers and pleasure boats which make gentle progress along its tranquil route. The cruisers no doubt welcome the fact that the Monmouthshire and Brecon was designed to follow the contours of the landscape, so locks are few and far between. Canal cruisers can be hired from a number of operators. For information on the canal please telephone (01873) 830328.

Monmouthshire and Brecon Canal near Gilwern

Blaenavon

If you want an accurate picture of coalmining in South Wales, then visit Blaenavon's Big Pit. Big Pit is not a contrived tourist experience: what you see here is an authentic coalmine, with all its rough edges, which has been preserved for posterity. Big Pit closed as a working mine in 1980, but reopened two years later as a mining museum. The surface workings are very much as they were – the workshops, engine house, pit-head baths and forge all look ready for business, as if the workers have just downed tools for the weekend.

But the undoubted highlight at Big Pit is the underground tour conducted by ex-miners. Visitors are equipped with helmets, cap lamps and safety batteries before descending 300 feet (90 m) by pit cage for a fascinating underground tour, which includes the coalface

and the stables where the horses – used for the heavy haulage – were kept. Open March–November daily 9.30–5 (underground tours 10–3.30). Telephone: (01495) 790311.

Across the valley, nearer to the town centre, are the Blaenavon Ironworks, dating from 1789. The blast furnaces here are exceptionally well preserved. A row of workers' cottages and an ingenious water balance lift are also part of this historically important site. Open May–September, Monday–Saturday 11–5, Sunday 2–5. Telephone: (01495) 792615.

Llancaiach Fawr, near Nelson

Living history is on the menu at Llancaiach Fawr. The period in question is Wales during the Civil War. From the moment you enter this Tudor manor house, you will be taken back in time by 'actor-

guides' who re-enact scenes from household life during the seventeenth century. The re-enactment is built around a visit made by King Charles I to the house in August 1645. It is all very convincingly done, and even the manners of the servants are in keeping with the period. The house itself is a rare survivor in Wales, a semi-fortified manor restored and furnished in the style of the seventeenth century. Open weekdays 10–5, Saturday 10–6, Sunday (March–October) 10–6, Sunday (October– March) 2–6. Telephone: (01443) 412248.

This road climbs across the empty moors of Mynydd Llangynidr and Mynydd Llangatwg into the Brecon Beacons National Park. Suddenly, you leave all signs of civilisation as you drive through a landscape reminiscent of wildest Scotland (interestingly, these moors were once used for grouse shooting). Within a few miles, the road crests a rise to reveal a marvellous panorama of the Brecon Beacons and Llangorse Lake, South Wales's largest natural lake. The road then drops down via hairpins to Llangynidr in the Usk Valley.

Turn right at the T-junction off the B4560 on to the B4558 on the outskirts of Llangynidr. Drive down the Usk Valley towards Crickhowell. This scenic, leafy road follows the course of the Monmouthshire and Brecon Canal, a waterway built between 1797 and 1812, now used by pleasure craft.

In about 3 ½ miles after Llangynidr, go straight on for

Gilwern at the traffic lights by the bridge which crosses the river into Crickhowell. (For a description of Crickhowell, please see Tour 4.)

Turn left in the centre of Gilwern, signposted Abergavenny ▣. In a further ¾ mile at the roundabout on the A465, take the B4269 for Govilon. After driving through Govilon, turn sharp right ▣ on to the B4246, signposted

Blaenavon.

The B4246 climbs steeply up the side of the Blorenge mountain to Blaenavon. This former industrial town preserves memories of the two elements – iron and coal – which changed the face of South Wales in the eighteenth and nineteenth centuries. As the 'B' road descends, on your right you will see Blaenavon Ironworks (Cadw-Welsh Historic Monuments),

Big Pit Mining Museum, Blaenavon, based at an authentic coalmine

open to visitors. But the town's most celebrated industrial monument is the Big Pit Mining Museum (signposted), standing in an exposed spot on the mountainside above and just to the west of the town. If you intend taking the underground tour at Big Pit, you will need to allocate at least two to three hours for the visit.

After visiting Big Pit, follow the A4043 south for Pontypool, another former metal-producing town. In the town's large and attractive parkland you can visit the Valley Inheritance, an interpretive centre based at the former stable blocks of an old mansion which tells the story of the great changes that occurred here during industrial times.

From Pontypool, take the A472 westwards to Crumlin in the Ebbw Valley. At Crumlin, take the A467 south for just over a mile to Newbridge, where you join the A472 for Ystrad Mynach in the Rhymney Valley. Stay on this road through Ystrad Mynach for Nelson. (For a fuller description of the route between Newbridge and Ystrad Mynach, see Tour 2.)

At the roundabout on the southern approach to Nelson D, turn off the A472 along the B4255 for the centre of the village and Llancaiach Fawr Historic House. In the centre, stay on the B4255, going straight on in the direction of Bedlinog, and in about ³/₄ mile at Trelewis turn right on to the B4254 for Gelligaer. Llancaiach Fawr is shortly on your right.

After visiting Llancaiach Fawr, drive along the B4254 to the outskirts of Gelligaer. If you want to see Gelligaer's scant Roman remnants, proceed into the village. Otherwise turn left on to a minor road (signposted Dowlais, Fochriw) which takes you past the Cross Inn

Valley Inheritance, Pontypool

and on to the mountain route northwards.

Gelligaer still bears traces of its ancestry as a Roman auxiliary fort, which was maintained more or less continuously until the Romans' withdrawal from Wales in the fourth century. The fort's rectangular earthworks are reasonably well preserved in archaeological terms. They can be seen in a field in the centre of the village.

In just over a mile after the Cross Inn, the road reaches open common land. Go straight on here heading northwards, and in another mile go straight on at the crossroads, staying on the main route northwards across the mountain for a few miles. The Romans' camps were connected by well-engineered roads which usually stuck to high ground for defensive reasons. You are now following the approximate course of the Roman road which ran along the moorland ridge from Gelligaer to Fochriw, part of the route between their forts in Cardiff and Brecon. **When you come to the road junction just after the Mount Pleasant Inn, bear left, then go immediately right down the hill into Fochriw.**

Continue on the road from Fochriw E towards Rhymney, a former coal and iron town. The road descends into the bottom of the valley, where you turn left on to the A469 for Merthyr Tydfil.

Just before the A469 joins the A465 'Heads of the Valleys' road, take a short detour into Butetown, signposted Drenewydd Museum. In an area characterised by its tightly packed terraced housing, Butetown comes as a refreshing surprise. It is a 'model village', well designed and neatly laid out, built by a philanthropic ironmaster for his workers in 1802–3. The village of attractive two- and three-storey dwellings has been sympathetically restored, and two of the former cottages have been converted into a local museum.

After visiting Butetown, return to Merthyr by the A465. ■

Cyfarthfa Castle, Merthyr Tydfil

THE BRECON BEACONS

44 MILES – 2 ½ HOURS
START AND FINISH AT BRECON

This tour takes you through the heart of the Brecon Beacons National Park. First stop out of Brecon is the Mountain Centre, an excellent introduction to the national park and its outdoor activities. This is a good tour for walkers, for there are many opportunities for mountain and forest walks along the way. The lakes of South Wales also feature strongly. The route runs beside scenic reservoirs as well as calling at the beautiful natural lake at Llangorse.

From the centre of Brecon, follow the one-way system westwards, turning left at the traffic lights just after the cinema. The road crosses the River Usk and in about ¾ mile brings you to the roundabout at the western outskirts of the town.

At the roundabout **A** take the minor road signposted Distillery Visitor Centre and Mynydd Illtyd (do not take the A470 south signposted National Park Visitor Centre). Follow this minor road, which climbs through country lanes to the open spaces of Mynydd Illtyd common.

The common is named after the influential Celtic religious leader, St Illtyd, who was instrumental in bringing Christianity to Wales in the fifth century. He was traditionally thought to be buried on the common at Bedd Illtyd, a site marked by a collection of large stones in a shallow pit, though nowadays his body is believed to be elsewhere, possibly at Llantwit Major, where he founded a monastic community (see Tour 3). It is no accident that the road across the common is straight as a die. This is part of the Roman Road of Sarn Helen which ran to the fort of Y Gaer on the western approach to Brecon.

In just over 4 miles from the roundabout on Brecon's outskirts, turn left for the National Park Visitor Centre (signposted Mountain Centre on a small wooden sign). Follow the winding country lane past the farmhouse for just over ½ mile to the Visitor Centre car park. After your visit, follow the minor road down the hillside (signposted Merthyr Tydfil) to Libanus and the A470, where you turn right for Merthyr Tydfil.

The A470 south through the Beacons is an outstandingly scenic road. It cuts between two mountain ranges, with Fforest Fawr on your right and the central

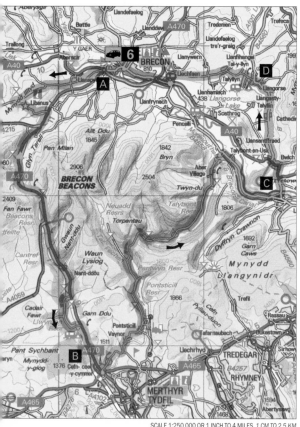

SCALE 1:250 000 OR 1 INCH TO 4 MILES *1 CM TO 2.5 KM*

Brecon Beacons Mountain Centre

Beacons on your left. Storey Arms, at the 1,440-foot (439 m) summit of the pass, is a favourite stopping-off place with plenty of car parking. Do not expect any catering or refreshment facilities though, for the 'Arms' is an outdoor pursuits centre. It was named after landowner Storey Maskelyne and, despite its title, has never served a pint of beer in its life.

The licensed premises here once stood at Pont ar Daf, about ½ mile further along the A470 from Storey Arms. This is another popular spot with good car parking. A well-trodden footpath leads from the roadside to the summits of Pen y Fan and Corn Du.

From Pont ar Daf, stay on the A470 south. Shortly, the first of a string of three reservoirs will come into view. They were created between 1892 and 1927 to supply the growing town of Cardiff, taking advantage of the high rainfall (up to 100 inches/254 cm a year) in these parts. After the Beacons reservoir comes Cantref reservoir.

At the northern end of the third, Llwyn-on reservoir, turn right on to the minor

---

• PLACES OF INTEREST •

Brecon

This town, beside the River Usk, is a natural base from which to explore the 519 square miles of the Brecon Beacons National Park. It is centrally located beneath the main peaks of the Beacons, and has a good choice of accommodation, ranging from town-centre inns and hotels to outlying farmhouses. In the main car park next to the cattle market there is a large Tourist Information Centre.

Brecon's livelihood stems from a combination of farming, administration and tourism. The farming community comes to town on Tuesday and Friday for the livestock sales, and there is also a general market in a covered market hall where you can buy everything from Welsh cheeses to clothes pegs. The big annual event which brings in thousands of visitors is Brecon Jazz, a major summer festival which attracts top musicians from all over the world.

The town's narrow streets fan out from the central square known as The Bulwark, dominated by a statue of Wellington and the tall tower, in local sandstone, of St Mary's Church. Around and about you will find plentiful evidence of Brecon's fashionable Georgian era in the form of well-proportioned

façades and a splendid Guildhall of 1770.

At one approach to The Bulwark stands the old Shire Hall, a magnificent white-stoned building in classical style, complete with a grand portico. This is now the home of the Brecknock Museum, one of the main features of which is a perfectly preserved Victorian assize court. The museum is also famous for its collection of Welsh lovespoons, intricately carved from solid blocks of wood and given as a symbol of betrothal in the rural Wales of bygone times. This attractive museum covers a lot of ground, from Roman artefacts to agricultural equipment. Open all year, Monday–Friday 10–5, Saturday 10–1 and 2–5. Sunday (April–September only) 10–1 and 2–5. Telephone: (01874) 624121.

Brecon's other museum, dedicated to South Wales Borderers, is at the army's headquarters along the Watton. This museum is a must for military fans and anyone who is interested in the Zulu Wars during which, in 1879, the regiment was involved in the heroic defence of Rorke's Drift. Open April–September daily 9–5. Telephone: (01874) 613310.

Up on the hill, fragments of Brecon's ruined medieval stronghold are now part of the Castle Hotel. A little further along is Brecon Cathedral, a vast medieval church which assumed cathedral status in 1923, serving a large diocese. A religious site was founded here in the twelfth century, at the same time as the castle. Although restored in the 1870s, many earlier features remain, including a Norman font and Early English chancel arch. The cathedral's history is explained in its Heritage Centre.

From the bridge over the Usk a pleasant riverside walk, with views of the Beacons, leads to a pavilion where you can hire boats. On the western approach to the town is a distillery, open to the public, with an entertaining attraction – the Welsh Whisky Experience – which traces the history of whisky-making in Wales.

Brecon Beacons Mountain Centre, near Libanus

If you are interested in the many outdoor opportunities that are offered by the Brecon Beacons National Park, then call into this centre. Or, as many of its visitors do, come simply to see the views, for the centre enjoys a wonderful location, high up on Mynydd Illtyd, looking out across the Tarrell Valley to the distinctive, flat-topped summit of Pen y Fan. At 2,907 feet (886 m), it is the highest peak in South Wales. The purpose-built centre contains maps and models of the park, while outside, below the terraces, there is a large grassy area. From the centre, there are easy walks to follow along the gently undulating common of Mynydd Illtyd. Open daily 9.30–5 (4.30 in winter). Telephone: (01874) 623366.

Llangorse

The village of Llangorse lies in a basin of land, flanked by steep hills, just north of the lake of the same name. The church in the centre of the village has an ancient pedigree. Although largely Norman in design it was founded much earlier, by St Paulinus, a tutor to St David. The church's pre-medieval origins have been further substantiated by the discovery here of a Viking burial stone. Llangorse Lake, over 1 mile long by ½ mile wide, is the largest natural lake in South Wales and has inspired many a legend, including that of the inevitable sunken city. Historians are on firmer ground when they speak of a prehistoric settlement of lake dwellers here. A tiny artificial island, built up as a stockade by early settlers, still exists.

road (signposted Garwnant Forest Centre – the entry to the Forest Centre is shortly on your right).

Wood, as well as water, has been introduced by man to the southern slopes of the Beacons. The Coed Taf Fawr woodlands around Llwyn-on are typical of the many Forestry Commission conifer plantations to be found in the national park. The purpose-built centre at Garwnant is a focal point for information on the wildlife and landscapes of the

forests. It is also the starting point for a number of waymarked woodland routes, and boasts a large and imaginative forest play area popular with children.

On leaving Garwnant, take the minor road around the western shore of the reservoir, cross the top of the dam and rejoin the A470 southwards on the eastern side of the valley.

At the time of writing, a new road is being constructed a few miles south of the reservoir; this

will carry the A470 across the valley, bypassing Cefn-Coed-y-cymmer and Merthyr Tydfil. **You need to stay on the road south into Cefn-Coed-y-cymmer, then turn left  on to the minor road signposted Pontsticill and Talybont immediately before the bridge over the A465.**

Follow the minor road through Pontsticill and over the mountains to Talybont-on-Usk. At Pontsticill you can take a short detour across the top of the reservoir dam to the terminus of the narrow-gauge Brecon Mountain Railway, which travels from the northern end of Merthyr Tydfil (for details see Tour 5).

From Pontsticill, the road runs through more forestry plantations with good leisure facilities – car parking, picnic sites and forest walks.

Within about 3 miles of Pontsticill, the road climbs up a mountain pass known locally as the Glyn. At the top of the Glyn, just before the very sharp downhill right-hand bend, take the road to the left for the Forest Car Park. This is the start of a very

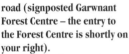

Downstream from the Blaen-y-glyn waterfall

attractive walk leading to the Blaen-y-glyn waterfall which tumbles down a rocky, wooded course from the heights of the Beacons.

Take care when driving down the steep and sometimes narrow road from the summit of the Glyn. You shortly come to the headwaters of the Talybont reservoir, a large lake which supplies Newport. The road runs along the shores of the reservoir, a nature reserve noted for its wildfowl, then through the hamlet of Aber to Talybont (NB. less than a mile after Aber bear right into Talybont: do not go straight on).

Immediately after crossing over the Monmouthshire and Brecon Canal at Talybont-on-Usk, turn right on to the B4558 for Llangynidr. The River Usk at Talybont is not to be found in the village itself, as the name implies, but across the fields. Talybont does lie on another important waterway, the Monmouthshire and Brecon Canal (see Tour 5 for details). The village is a pleasant spot in which to enjoy a walk along the canal towpath or refreshment at one of a good choice of country pubs.

From Talybont, drive to Llangynidr, where you should bear left ◖C◗ off the B4558 as it crosses the canal just before the Coach and Horses pub, signposted Lower Llangynidr and Bwlch. In approximately ½ mile, turn left at the T-junction and shortly cross the very narrow bridge over the river (caution). Climb the hill and turn left on to the A40. Drive through Bwlch, and turn right by the monument along the B4560 for Llangorse, with views of the lake on your left. Pass the church and Red Lion Hotel in the centre of Llangorse and shortly turn left ◖D◗, signposted Brecon and Llangorse Lake. In a short distance take a small detour left to Llangorse Lake (signposted).

After visiting the lake, return to the road for Brecon, drive through Llanfihangel Tal-y-llyn and continue on the road towards Brecon for a couple of miles until you come to a T-junction on the outskirts of Groesffordd. Turn left here, drive under the bridge carrying the A40 and turn immediately right to join the A40 dual-carriageway for Brecon. ■

Pen-y-Fan, the summit of the Beacons

BRECON BEACONS WATERFALL COUNTRY

38 MILES – 2 HOURS
START AND FINISH AT GLYN NEATH

The Brecon Beacons National Park is not all hill and mountain. Although parts of this tour take you through highland South Wales, it concentrates on the waterfalls, ravines and caves of the national park's limestone country, a distinctive little corner of the Brecon Beacons. You can even take a look underground at the popular Dan-yr-Ogof Showcaves, an extensive cave system open to the public. This is another tour which walkers will enjoy, with a choice of paths short and long to spectacular waterfalls.

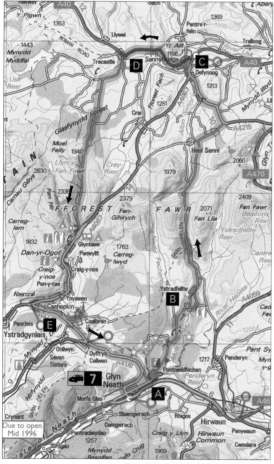

SCALE 1:250 000 OR 1 INCH TO 4 MILES *1 CM TO 2.5 KM*

This tour starts in the Vale of Neath, a valley that has seen many changes for the better in the last decade or so. With the decline of coalmining, landscaping and environmental improvement schemes have returned much of the valley to its former attractiveness.

Glyn Neath is a small community at the head of the valley just off the A465 Merthyr Tydfil to Swansea road. **Leave Glyn Neath on the B4242 in the direction of Pontneddfechan. In just after a mile (a short distance after the Tourist Information Centre), turn left A up the hill for the minor road to Ystradfellte.**

Although at the start of this tour, you should at least consider stopping off at Pontneddfechan to follow the well-surfaced footpath northwards from the bridge in the village, which leads beside the banks of the River Neath to its junction with the River Pyrddin. Bear left here along the Pyrddin and in a short distance you will come to the beautiful waterfall of Sgwd Gwladus, also known as the Lady's Fall. The entire walk, there and back, is only 2½ miles.

Ystradfellte's waterfall country

Sgwd Gwladus serves as an introduction to a strange part of the Brecon Beacons National Park, the limestone country on which this tour concentrates. The park is predominantly a highland area of old red sandstone, a rock which has weathered to produce a landscape of empty moors and smooth-flanked mountains. The only exception to this geological rule lies along the park's southern boundary, where a band of limestone outcrops creates a jagged, jumbled terrain of rocky gorges, wooded ravines, caves and waterfalls.

The hamlet of Ystradfellte lies at the heart of this limestone country. **Half a mile before reaching Ystradfellte, turn right B down the narrow road (after the Youth Hostel) for Porth-yr-Ogof Cave.** There is a large car park here, directly above the cave entrance.

After visiting Porth-yr-Ogof and Waterfall Country continue on the minor road for just over ¼ mile, turning left at the T-junction. This road brings you into the hamlet of Ystradfellte, where you turn right and drive north

---

• *PLACES OF INTEREST* •

Porth-yr-Ogof, Ystradfellte
Porth-yr-Ogof ('The Gateway to the Cave') is one of the most famous caves in South Wales. The cave entrance, a gaping mouth at the base of a shady cliff, is reputedly the largest in Wales. It swallows the River Mellte, which reappears ¼ mile downstream. Porth-yr-Ogof is a classic limestone cavern, caused by the action of water on this easily soluble rock. The river course also displays many textbook examples of limestone scenery. There are gurgling pot-holes everywhere, and in dry weather its waters disappear completely beneath ground, leaving an empty, boulder-strewn riverbed. When the waters are low, you can venture a short distance into the cave entrance to pick out

the white formation on the rock, resembling a horse, which gives the cave its alternative name of 'White Horse Cavern'. Do not be tempted to venture far: caving is a serious, potentially dangerous business, reserved for the parties of well-equipped cavers who flock to this compelling spot.

Waterfall Country
South Wales's classic waterfalls are to be found downstream of Porth-yr-Ogof on the Mellte and Hepste rivers. From the Porth-yr-Ogof car park, follow the path south across rough ground. Having run underground through the cave system, the Mellte reappears in a deep and dangerous pool. From here, a pleasant riverbank path leads within less than a mile to

Sgwd Clun-Gwyn ('White Meadow Fall'), the first of a series of spectacular waterfalls set in a rocky, wooded gorge. A little further downstream are Sgwd Isaf Clun-Gwyn ('Lower White Meadow Fall') and Sgwd y Pannwr ('The Fall of the Fuller'). Sgwd yr Eira ('The Spout of Snow'), the most famous of the falls, is on the Hepste, a tributary of the Mellte which joins the river about ¼ mile downstream from Sgwd y Pannwr. At Sgwd yr Eira, a curtain of water drops 50–60 feet (15–18 m), and you can enjoy the experience of walking behind the waterfall and not getting wet by following a path on the ledge beneath the overhang. The entire walk there and back from the Porth-yr-Ogof car park to Sgwd yr Eira is about 4 ½ miles.

Dan-yr-Ogof Showcaves, near Abercraf

These caverns, a major South Wales tourist attraction, claim to be the largest showcaves complex in western Europe. The entrance, high on a hill beneath craggy limestone outcrops, leads to three separate cave experiences. Most popular is the main Showcave, in which visitors see weird stalagmite and stalactite formations on a walk through the first ½ mile of a labyrinthine network of passages, extending many miles undergound, which was first discovered in 1912. The Cathedral Cave is so called because of the 'Dome of St Paul's', a huge cavern reached by a long passageway. Cave settlement and archeology are the themes within the educational Bone Cave. The complex has much to interest all ages, including a Dinosaur Park and dry ski slope. Open April–October daily 10–4. Telephone: (01639) 730284.

Craig-y-nos Country Park

These landscaped grounds beside the River Tawe were created as an accompaniment to Craig-y-nos Castle, home of the internationally acclaimed nineteenth-century opera star Madame Adelina Patti. Her 'pleasure grounds', covering 40 acres (16 hectares), contain meadows, lakes and woods. It is managed by the Brecon Beacons National Park. Open daily at all reasonable hours. Telephone: (01639) 730395.

along the mountain road across Fforest Fawr.

Do not expect to see many trees when travelling through these brooding, uninhabited moorlands. The 'forest' title harks back to medieval times when the term described not woodland but an area used for hunting. Fforest Fawr, the 'Great Forest' of Brecknock, was a royal hunting ground prized for its deer and wild boar.

The narrow mountain road follows part of the old Sarn Helen Roman road on its way northwards across the bare, boggy moorland. On your left, just before the high point in the road, you will see the solitary standing stone of Maen Llia, a survivor from the Bronze Age and the best example of a single standing stone in the Brecon Beacons. Around 12 feet (3.5 m) tall and tapering to a sharp point, it may possibly have been a monument to ancient spirits. A less colourful theory has it serving as a route marker.

From the 1,470-foot (448 m) summit, there are splendid views northwards across the Senni Valley and surrounding mountains. **The road now descends steeply via hairpin bends, then follows the eastern flank of the Senni Valley. At the T-junction near Heol Senni, turn right, then left along the A4215 for Defynnog and Sennybridge in the Usk Valley.**

At the junction of the A4215 and A4067 turn right C. In less than ½ mile turn left into Sennybridge (do not go straight on for the A40 eastbound). The road leads to the main part of the village where you will join the A40 (westbound), turning left for Trecastle.

The A40 runs along the northern boundary of the Brecon Beacons National Park. To the north are the bleak and inhospitable military training ranges of Mynydd Eppynt.

Turn left by the Castle Coaching Inn in the centre of Trecastle D. The road drops down the hill to a bridge, where you bear right (staying on the 'main' road). One mile after crossing the bridge, turn

High in the Black Mountain

High in the Black Mountain

left for the road south through the Glasfynydd Forest, signposted Abercraf and Tafarn-y-Garreg.

Skirting the wildernesses of the Black Mountain, this is another memorable upland route. **Follow the road south to the A4067 in the upper Tawe Valley, where you turn right. Shortly, you will come to the entrance**

to the Dan-yr-Ogof Showcaves on your right. After visiting the caves, you can also call into the Craig-y-nos Country Park (entrance and car park shortly on your left).

Continue along the A4067, turning left on to the A4221 at Abercraf. The road climbs up to a plateau and the old coalmining community of Coelbren.

Turn left E off the A4221 at Coelbren for a short detour to the Henrhyd Falls (National Trust), located on the northern fringe of the village. The Henrhyd Falls are the most easily accessible of all the waterfalls featured on this tour. Follow the path down into the gorge from the car park to view the unbroken 90-foot (27 m) cascade of water. Thin seams of coal outcrop on the cliffs around the falls, evidence of the start of the coal seams which underlie industrial South Wales.

Return to the A4221, which shortly joins the A4109 back to Glyn Neath. ∎

Henrhyd Falls, Coelbren

THE WESTERN VALLEYS

52 MILES – 2 ½ HOURS
START AND FINISH AT NEATH

On the face of it, a history of coalmining and the presence of intense natural beauty do not seem to go together. Yet, on this tour, you will become acquainted with both. The splendid grounds of Margam Park are the first treat, followed by a scenic route through vale and over mountain to the Rhondda. A forested country park, home of a mining museum, neatly encapsulates the double-sided personality of 'industrial' South Wales. The Vale of Neath is another surprisingly attractive valley, with canal walks, waterfalls and a noted wildlife park.

• PLACES OF INTEREST •

Neath
This former industrial town stands at the gateway to the attractive Vale of Neath. Excavations in 1949 uncovered the long-suspected Roman fort of *Nidum*. Neath's location was also favoured by medieval conquerors, as witnessed by the remains of a thirteenth-century castle. The castle stands close to the town centre, a pedestrianised area with a Victorian covered market selling fresh produce and Welsh fare such as laverbread. The Neath Borough Museum, housed in a beautiful nineteenth-century building that was once the home of a man who worked with Darwin on his theory of evolution, tells the story of Neath's varied history. Open Tuesday–Saturday 10–4. Telephone: (01639) 645741.

Neath Abbey (Cadw-Welsh Historical Monuments), located on the banks of the Tennant Canal, was described as the 'fairest abbey in all Wales' by Tudor historian John Leland. Founded in 1130 and later absorbed into the Cistercian order, it has an unusual post-religious history. Following the Dissolution of the Monasteries in the sixteenth century, the south-eastern part of the cloister ranges was converted into a grand

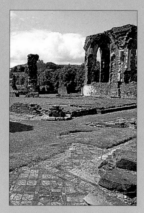

mansion. The ruins then suffered the indignity of being used for copper smelting when furnaces were established in the west range. Free access. Open at all reasonable times.

The Gnoll Estate Country Park on the Neath–Tonna road is based on an eighteenth-century landscaped garden. It contains cascades, grottos, forest footpaths, an ice house, children's play area and adventure playground. Open dawn to dusk. Telephone: (01639) 635808.

Margam Park
This beautiful park, comprising 850 acres (344 hectares) of open parkland and forest, is full of historic and natural treasures as well as fun attractions. Margam Castle was built as a home for local magnates, the Talbots. It is an impressive Tudor/Gothic mansion completed in 1840 and partially restored following a fire in 1977. The park also contains an Iron Age hill fort and the remains of a twelfth-century Cistercian abbey. The most impressive building in the park is the magnificent and fully restored Margam Orangery, constructed in 1789 to house orange and lemon trees.

Family attractions within the park include a scaled-down 'nursery rhyme' village, boating lake, pets' corner, fallow deer herd and farm trail. There is also one of the largest conifer mazes in Europe. During the summer, access can be gained to the Abbey Stones Museum (Cadw-Welsh Historic Monuments), located alongside the Abbey Church of St Mary, just outside the park, which houses a collection of early Christian and pagan stones. Country park open April–September daily 10–7 (attractions 10–5). October–March, Wednesday–Sunday 10–5 (country park only). Telephone: (01639) 881635.

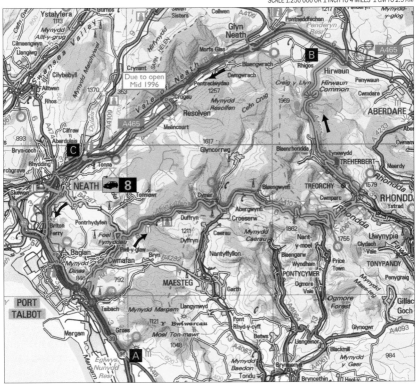

Neath stands close to the mouth of the river of the same name. Although it has shrugged off its copper smelting past, it retains a traditional look and atmosphere – not to mention strong love of rugby (the town is proud of the fact that the Welsh Rugby Union was formed here at the Castle Hotel on 12 March 1881). **Leave Neath on the A474 southwards, joining the M4 eastbound (for Bridgend and Cardiff) at Baglan.**

The motorway runs on a shelf of land between steep hillsides and a coastal plain almost entirely filled with the town and steelworks of Port Talbot, home-town of actor Sir Anthony Hopkins. Port Talbot takes its name from the pre-eminent local family, the Talbots of Margam, who established docks here for the export of coal and metal. Aberavon, Port Talbot's seafront neighbour, seems a strange place in which to have a seaside resort – though admittedly the huge stretch of sands and long promenade are nowadays frequented only by day-visitors (the resort's heyday was in the earlier part of the twentieth century, when people poured in from the nearby industrial valleys).

Leave the M4 at junction 38 A, taking the A48 towards Pyle. The entrance to Margam Park is shortly on the left. After visiting the park, travel back up the motorway towards Neath and Swansea, leaving the M4 at junction 40 for the A4107. Drive along the A4107 through the Afan Valley.

The Afan Valley is perhaps the best example in South Wales of the changing relationship between natural beauty and industrial exploitation. Although once riddled with coalmines, this narrow, winding valley is known as 'Little Switzerland'. Extensive conifer plantations cover the hillsides and old industrial sites have been removed, creating an extremely pleasant scene.

There must be something in the water in these parts, for no

Margam Park

43

Afan Argoed Country Park

Turn left at the T-junction in the middle of Treorchy, following the A4061 north through Treherbert and up over another mountain to Hirwaun.

As you drive up the valley, one town blends into the next. Tonypandy becomes Llwynypia becomes Ton Pentre becomes Treorchy becomes Treherbert. You will look in vain for any sign of coalmines. (If you have time you can take a detour off this route southwards for about 3 miles down the valley from Tonypandy to Trehafod, between Porth and Pontypridd, where the old Lewis Merthyr colliery is now the site of the Rhondda Heritage Park, a museum dedicated to coalmining.)

After Treherbert, the road climbs out of the valley along the scenic Rhigos mountain road, built by out-of-work miners in the 1930s. At the summit there is another car park and viewpoint at about 1,600 feet (488 m), this time with stunning vistas northwards across the Brecon Beacons to Mid Wales. The road descends towards Hirwaun via looping bends past the glacial lake of Llyn Fawr, tucked in beneath a precipitous escarpment. The colliery beside the road has the distinction of being the only working coalmine left in South Wales, a profitable pit which survived because of a buy-out by its enterprising miners.

At the bottom of the mountain road you will come to a roundabout B, where you take the turning south-eastwards to Hirwaun, staying on the A4061. After just over ½ mile, turn on to the A465 at the major roundabout in the direction of Swansea.

The A465 dual-carriageway road drops down into the Vale of Neath and the little town of Glyn Neath (for information on Glyn Neath and Pontneddfechan, see Tour 7). This attractive valley has been the scene of much environmental improvement,

more than a handful of miles from Port Talbot, just off the A4107 at its junction with the B4287 to Neath, is the village of Pontrhydyfen, birthplace of that other great Welsh actor, Richard Burton.

A mile or so further along the valley from the Pontrhydyfen turn-off, turn right for the Afan Argoed Country Park and Welsh Miners' Museum (signposted).

After visiting the park and museum, continue along the A4107 through Cymer. After Cymer, the road begins to climb across the wild and exposed top of the mountain which separates the Afan from the Rhondda valleys.

Turn left where the A4107 joins the A4061 and stop in the car park to gaze down into the Rhondda, its rows of terraced houses looking like a toy town from this height and distance. From here,

follow the A4061 down to Treorchy in the Rhondda Fawr Valley.

Of all the valleys in South Wales, the Rhondda is the best known (in fact, there are two Rhondda valleys – the 'big' Rhondda, the Rhondda Fawr featured on this tour, and the 'little' Rhondda, Rhondda Fach, in a separate valley to the east). Both were famous for the coal – the 'black diamond' – mined here, and for the spirited communities which grew up, sharing common hardship in the tightly packed terraces where miners and their families lived.

It is almost unbelievable to contemplate that as late as the mid-nineteenth century, the Rhondda was almost untouched by industry. The growth, when it came, was explosive. Coalmines were sunk all along the valley, and a series of pit villages grew up in long, thin lines, filling the narrow valley floor because of the restrictions on space.

Treorchy in the Rhondda Fawr Valley

44

• PLACES OF INTEREST •

Afan Argoed Country Park and Welsh Miners' Museum

This park, set in a beautiful steep-sided forested valley, can be explored in a variety of ways: on foot, by bike (cycle hire available), or on a Land Rover tour from the main car park. Easy-to-follow waymarked trails fan out through the forest from the park's countryside centre.

For many, the highlight of a visit to Afan Argoed is the award-winning South Wales Miners' Museum. Created by ex-colliers, the museum portrays the mining industry through the eyes of those who worked in it, telling of the struggles, hardship, community spirit and warmth of the mining communities of the South Wales valleys. Old photographs, mining equipment, a scene from a miner's cottage and simulated underground workings help bring to life the dangers and dignity of mining. Country park open dawn to dusk. Countryside centre and museum open April–September, daily 10.30–6. October–March, daily 10.30–4. Telephone: (01639) 850564.

Aberdulais Falls

After a short walk along the River Dulais, a wooded gorge reveals one of the most celebrated waterfalls in Wales. Since 1584, its waters have been harnessed to provide power for a variety of industries from copper smelting to tinplate workings. Yet the falls still possess a great natural beauty, and have attracted the attention of many artists.

Located here today is one of Europe's largest electricity-generating waterwheels, part of a unique hydro-electricity scheme. Other features at this fascinating National Trust site include an interactive display for visitors and guided tours (in the summer months). Open April–October, Monday–Friday 10–5, Saturday and Sunday 11–6. Telephone: (01639) 636674.

Penscynor Wildlife Park, near Neath

This 16-acre (6-hectare) park contains some of the world's most endangered and beautiful animals, including 100 species of exotic bird and 25 species of monkey as well as a small aquarium, reptile house, deer and otters. Highlights include feeding time for the chimps and penguins, talks, tours and handling sessions. In addition to the wildlife, the popular park has a chairlift and toboggan alpine slide, radio-controlled boats and cars, and a children's playground. Open April–September, daily 10–6, October–March, daily 10–4. Telephone: (01639) 642189.

especially along the banks of the Neath Canal. Before the turn-off to Resolven, the A465 runs alongside the canal. There are boat trips on the restored waterway from the basin at Resolven, and tranquil towpath trails for walkers.

Turn left off the A465 on to the B4434 at Resolven. Stay on the 'B' road for Tonna, rejoining the A465 at Aberdulais. Just after Resolven, you can take a short detour left for the waterfalls at Melincourt. These are some of the largest and also most easily accessible falls in South Wales. The site is a nature reserve owned by the Glamorgan Wildlife Trust.

Aberdulais is full of interest, both scenic and industrial. The canal basin here is noted for its skew bridge and 12-arched aqueduct, though the main focus of attention is a National Trust site, the wonderful Aberdulais Falls. **The falls are located almost at the junction of the B4434 and A465 C. After visiting the falls, drive along the A465 a short distance in the direction of Neath. Turn off at the roundabout for the Penscynor Wildlife Park (signposted a short distance north of the roundabout).** Penscynor, one of South Wales's top tourist attractions, is a great favourite with children. **After visiting the park, rejoin the A465 for the journey back to Neath.** ∎

Llyn Fawr, at the northern gateway to the Rhondda

45

SWANSEA AND THE GOWER PENINSULA

49 MILES – 2 ½ HOURS
START AND FINISH AT SWANSEA CITY CENTRE

Swansea, Wales's second city, is the base for this tour of contrasts. This maritime city, an appealing mixture of modern and traditional influences, enjoys a fortunate location on a wide, sandy bay. Moreover, it stands close to the shores of the magnificent Gower Peninsula, where development is tightly controlled. Within a few minutes of Swansea are the beaches and headland walks, cliffs and hidden coves of south Gower. There are more contrasts along Gower's northern shores bordering the Loughor Estuary, a bleakly beautiful area of saltings and cockle beds.

Unlike Cardiff, where the waterfront is a mile or so from the city centre, Swansea is a true city-by-the-sea. The great arc of Swansea Bay, the 'long and splendid curving shore' described by Dylan Thomas, the city's most famous son, is only a stone's throw from the busy shopping centre.

The first few miles of this tour follow the A4067 coast road along the Swansea Bay to The Mumbles. On the way, you will pass Singleton Park and the university campus.

The Mumbles is part sailing centre, part seaside resort and part coastal town. An attractive seafront walk alongside the boat park leads up to Mumbles Head, a rocky promontory with a pier, amusements and small beach. The resort's unusual name is thought to originate from the French *mamelles* ('breasts'), a reference to the two islets off the headland which are accessible at low tide.

After visiting Mumbles Head, retrace your route a mile back to Oystermouth, turning left A on to the B4593 for Langland Bay and Caswell Bay.

Oystermouth, which blends into The Mumbles, is home to an unusually well-preserved castle (Cadw-Welsh Historic Monuments) built on a grassy rise overlooking the bay. Dating from 1280, it acted both as a stronghold and comfortable home. Its beautifully decorated and pointed windows are an exceptional feature.

Oystermouth and The Mumbles stand at the gateway to the Gower Peninsula, a stubby, lovely promontory about 18 miles long. In 1955, it was the first part of Britain to be declared an official 'Area of Outstanding Natural Beauty'.

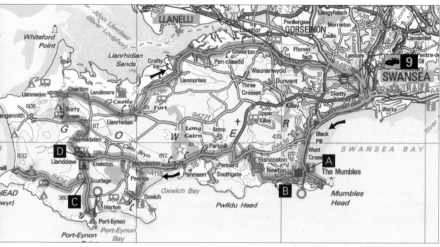

SCALE 1:250 000 OR 1 INCH TO 4 MILES *1 CM TO 2.5 KM*

The Mumbles, at the gateway to Gower

Gower's southern shore is made up of towering headlands, cliffs and sheltered south-facing bays, many with unspoilt sandy beaches. Car parking can become a problem on busy summer weekends and Bank Holidays, especially at popular spots close to the city such as Langland and Caswell. In season, weekdays are a much better option for exploring the coastal glories of this delightful little peninsula.

Caswell Bay, the 'Jewel of Gower', has a large car park next to its big beach. The far end of the car park leads into Bishop's Wood Nature Reserve, a secluded, wooded valley running inland. Walkers can also follow coastal paths at Caswell. A westward path leads to the old smugglers' haunt of Brandy Cove, while the path to the east goes around the headland back to Langland Bay.

From Caswell Bay ◼B, proceed to Bishopston, turning left on to the B4436 which brings you to the A4118, where you turn left for Parkmill. Gower displays plentiful evidence of ancient settlement. One of its most outstanding prehistoric sites can be seen in countryside just north-west of Parkmill. Parc le Breos Burial Chamber (Cadw-Welsh Historic Monuments) is a sizeable neolithic stone tomb, around 70 feet (21 m) long, built around 4000–3500 BC for the communal burial of the dead. A little further along the valley is the entrance to Cathole Cave, an even older site which provided human shelter at the end of the Ice Age 10,000 years ago and in which flint tools and bones of mammoth and

---

• PLACES OF INTEREST •

Swansea

Wales's second city is a refreshing blend of traditional and modern. Despite heavy bombing in World War II and the wholesale reconstruction of the city centre, traditional Swansea lives on in its daily covered market which boasts one of the best selections of fresh foods in Wales. These include welshcakes, local Pen-clawdd cockles and laverbread, that unique Welsh delicacy – a kind of puréed seaweed – which is usually eaten with bacon. Swansea's Welshness is an essential part of its character: you are far more likely to hear Welsh being spoken in these streets than in Cardiff.

Swansea is also a modern and forward-looking city. It is home to a large university campus, and in the last few decades the city has been busily engaged on a new waterfront development which has attracted international architectural praise. Swansea's Maritime Quarter, based around the old docks, is an object lesson in how to bring new life to a run-down area. Its centrepiece is a

600-berth marina, lined with a residential quarter and a range of attractions. Amongst these is the city's Maritime and Industrial Museum, which tells the story of Swansea's development as a copper and tinplate manufacturer and exporter. The museum is housed in a former warehouse, so there is plenty of room for its most unusual exhibit – a fully operational woollen mill. Moored on the quay outside are a number of boats – including a lightship and steam tug – which are also part of the museum. Open Tuesday–Sunday 10.30–5.30. Telephone: (01792) 650351.

Gazing out over the marina is a statue of Dylan Thomas, who memorably described his home town as an 'ugly, lovely' place. The writer was born in the Uplands part of the city in 1914, next to the attractive Cwmdonkin Park, a place which featured in one of his early poems and now contains a memorial to Dylan.

Close to the new Maritime Quarter is Swansea's – and Wales' – oldest museum, founded in 1838. Amongst the encyclopaedic range of exhibits here is an exquisite collection of eighteenth- and nineteenth-century Swansea pottery and porcelain. Swansea's former role as an important ceramics centre is also reflected within the Glynn Vivian Art Gallery, founded by the wealthy Vivian industrialists in the early 1900s. Swansea's Guildhall of 1934 is noted for its magnificent panels on the theme of the British Empire. They were painted by Sir Frank Brangwyn and originally intended for the House of Lords.

The city's location on Swansea Bay can be appreciated by following a path and cycleway all the way along the seafront to The Mumbles 5 miles away.

Oxwich

You will approach Oxwich through a low-lying marshy area of tall reeds and rushes separated from the sea by a barrier of dunes. This varied habitat is protected as a National Nature Reserve, which can be explored by following waymarked paths from an information centre at the car park.

One path leads through the woods along the headland to Oxwich Point, passing the tiny Church of St Illtyd dating from the thirteenth century. Just above the village stands Oxwich Castle (Cadw-Welsh Historic Monuments), a sixteenth-century manor house, probably built on the site of an earlier castle, which gives an insight into the Tudor gentry's comfortable lifestyle. Open May–September 10–5.

Rhossili

Far-flung Rhossili is an inspiring spot. Steep, windswept cliffs tower above a vast, west-facing beach described by Dylan Thomas as 'miles of yellow coldness going away into the distance of the sea'. The cold does not seem to bother the surfers who congregate, whatever the weather, at Llangennith on the northern end of the beach to ride the biggest and best waves in South Wales. Look carefully on the beach and you will see the stumps of a ship which ran aground here in 1887. Rhossili itself is a cluster of dwellings at the base of a promontory which narrows into Worms Head. There is a memorable walk all the way along this crooked finger of land. But beware, for the Head is an island cut off from Rhossili at high tide – so check the tide times at the visitor centre before you set off. Rhossili's small church contains a memorial to local son Edgar Evans, better known as Petty Officer Evans, who perished on Captain Scott's second and ill-fated expedition to the Antarctic in 1912.

Weobley Castle, near Llanrhidian

Weobley's boxy defences overlook the haunting expanse of Llanrhidian Marsh. The site, dating from the late thirteenth century, is more fortified manor house than out-and-out castle. Substantial remains, including rooms large and small, kitchen and guest chamber, are set around a courtyard which is guarded by a gatehouse. Open summer daily 9.30–6.30, winter Monday–Saturday 9.30–4, Sunday 2–4. Telephone: (01792) 390012.

woolly rhinoceros have been found. Back in Parkmill, it is worth stopping off at Y Felin Ddŵr Craft and Countryside Centre, based at an old farm and watermill. From the village there are walks southwards across Pennard Burrows and beside the course of Pennard Pill to Three Cliffs Bay, one of the loveliest on Gower.

Continue on the A4118 from Parkmill, then in about 2½ miles turn left on to the minor road for Oxwich (signposted). The sandy bay at Oxwich is one of Gower's most popular spots. Except on very busy weekends, there is room enough for all, thanks to a large beach stretching over 2 miles and convenient seafront car parking at the southern end of the bay. **After visiting Oxwich, return along the road across the marsh to the A4118, turning left towards Port-Eynon. At the junction with the B4247 C,** stay on the A4118 for Port-Eynon.

Port-Eynon is another pretty sea-village, set on a rugged shoreline. It is worth spending some time in this old smugglers' haunt for, as well as the beach, there are fascinating places to visit within easy walking distance. Culver Hole, a short distance along the headland, is a strange walled-up section of cliff of mysterious origin. Close by are the ruins of the Salt House, a mansion reputedly destroyed by a great storm in 1703.

For the more energetic, the cliff walk between Port-Eynon and Rhossili is the most spectacular on Gower. The path skirts a remote coastline past the famous – though dangerously inaccessible – Paviland Cave where flint tools and the bones of an 18,000-year-old skeleton were discovered.

From Port-Eynon, return to the junction with the B4247, turning left along this road for Rhossili, Gower's wild

Oxwich Bay

'Land's End'. After visiting Rhossili, return to the A4118 and turn left. Turn off the A4118 at the sharp right-hand bend **D** in the road for the minor road in the direction of Llangennith.

Turn left at Burry Green, in ½ mile turning right for Cheriton, a pretty little village with a mid-thirteenth-century church. From Cheriton, follow the road eastwards past Landimore for Weobley Castle (Cadw-Welsh Historic Monuments).

Weobley Castle overlooks Gower's north coast, which represents a startling scenic contrast to the tall limestone cliffs along the southern shores of the peninsula. In the north, the coastline is an eerie mixture of marsh, saltings and huge stretches of low-tide sandflats.

Continue along the road to Llanrhidian, where you join the B4295 for Crofty, Pen-clawdd and Gowerton. Pen-clawdd is famous for its cockle beds and the hardy locals who venture out at low tide to pick the cockles, a tough, back-breaking job. Mechanisation cannot help. The cockles are picked by hand in the traditional way and loaded on to carts for sale in Swansea Market and elsewhere. For a true taste of Pen-clawdd, try them the traditional way, cooked and served cold in open paper bags, and eaten with a dash of vinegar.

Stay on the B4295 after Gowerton for about 3 miles, turning left briefly on to the A4216, then right along the A483 back to the centre of Swansea. ■

Pen-clawdd cockle-pickers

49

WILD WALES

34 MILES – 2 HOURS
START AND FINISH AT LLANDOVERY

Fans of Wild Wales, *the book written by nineteenth-century traveller George Borrow, should be particularly attracted to this tour. Borrow's classic book, still in print, recounts his tour of a largely undiscovered Wales. The 'wild' Wales of the title can still be found in the remote, unchanging Cambrian Mountains, the backbone of Wales which runs from south to north. This tour ventures into their southern foothills and takes in legendary sites associated with Twm Shôn Cati, the Robin Hood of Wales, and the Romans' search for Welsh gold.*

Llyn Brianne's massive dam

Borrow described Llandovery as 'the pleasantest little town in which I have halted in the course of my wanderings'. He stayed in the Castle Hotel, an old coaching inn beside a large car park in the centre of town.

From this car park, leave Llandovery on the A40 westbound, turning right by the railway station on to the A483 in the direction of Llanwrtyd Wells and Builth Wells. Within a short distance, turn left on to the minor road northwards for Rhandirmwyn (signposted).

Twenty or 30 years ago, this road northwards up the Tywi Valley saw little in the way of traffic. In those days, the route was a cul-de-sac for cars beyond the village of Rhandirmwyn, the surfaced road petering out into a rough track as it climbed into the mountains. Then came the

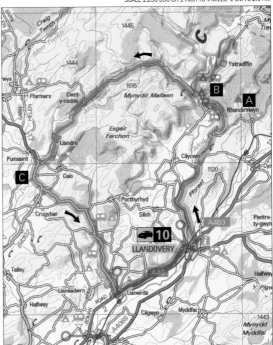

Llandovery

Llandovery – *Llanymyddyfi* ('The Church Amongst the Waters') in Welsh – fulfils all the criteria for a traditional Welsh country town. Llandovery's cobbled square and marketplace, surrounded by small shops and old inns, is dominated by a tall clocktower. There is plentiful evidence of Georgian façades, and at the back of the Castle Hotel a ruined medieval stronghold teeters on top of a steep mound. One of the buildings clustered around the clocktower has been tastefully converted into the excellent Dinefwr Crafts Centre, a collection of studios featuring work by local craftspeople.

Directly opposite the entrance to the Castle Hotel is the Tourist Information Centre. Imaginatively converted from eighteenth-century stables, it contains the Llandovery Heritage Centre which has exhibitions reflecting the history and legends of the Tywi Valley. Subjects covered include Twn Shôn Cati, the Welsh drovers, and the eighteenth-century hymn-

writer William Williams. The centre also contains information on local bird life.

The Romans built a fortress here to guard the river crossing and road to and from their goldmines at Dolaucothi. The site is now occupied by a large church with a tall thirteenth-century square tower. The town is home to Llandovery College, Wales's only Welsh-speaking public school. Llandovery holds a general market each Saturday, and a livestock market takes place here on alternate Tuesdays.

Dinas Hill and Twm Shôn Cati's Cave, Ystradffin

This is one of the most enchanting spots in all of South Wales. You will see Dinas Hill, a thickly wooded, conical hill, on your left as you drive up the Tywi Valley to the entrance and car park for the RSPB reserve, located just beyond the hill to the north. A footpath leads from the RSPB information centre down to the riverbank, where you pick up the start of a circular path around Dinas Hill.

Bear right here, taking the route along the river as it enters a rocky gorge, the Tywi tumbling over huge boulders and fierce rapids.

Bird life on the reserve is rich and varied, and includes buzzard, kestrel, sparrowhawk, raven, meadow pippit, skylark and pied flycatcher. But the bird that everyone wants to see in these parts is the rare red kite, which has made its home in the undisturbed hills around Llandovery.

Historically, Dinas Hill was also home to another elusive quarry. In the sixteenth century, an enigmatic character named Twm Shôn Cati, Wales's answer to Robin Hood, hid in a cave on the hill from the Sheriff of Carmarthen. His hideaway, amongst the boulders and oakwoods near the summit, is not easy to find – there is a path of sorts, which leads upwards before you come to the confluence of the Tywi and Doethi rivers. The search is worth it, not least for the initials and signatures carved by visitors in the cave walls dating back to the eighteenth century.

Dolaucothi Roman Goldmines, Pumsaint

These mines are the only ones in Britain where we know, for certain, that the Romans mined for gold. This precious metal was one of the reasons why they showed so much interest in Wales. Discovering gold deposits in the waters of the River Cothi, the Romans started serious mining operations here in AD75. The hillsides around Pumsaint became a thriving industrial site populated by thousands of slave workers. Pumsaint gold, one of Britain's most important exports in Roman times, was transported to the Imperial Mint at Lyon.

The area still displays evidence of the characteristically sophisticated technology and ingenuity employed by the Romans. Originally, they confined themselves to open-cast mining. Then came the tunnels and caverns which followed the gold-bearing seams of rock into the hillsides. Miles of aqueduct were painstakingly installed to assist in the extraction, washing and sorting of the gold. The Romans left in about AD200, and until another gold rush in the late nineteenth and early twentieth centuries, which was only partially successful, the mines lay abandoned and forgotten. They were finally closed in 1938. The mines are now owned by the National Trust, part of a 2,600-acre (1,052-hectare) holding known as the Dolaucothi Estate, which includes farmlands and the village of Pumsaint. Visitors can follow footpaths around the site and, in summer, join conducted underground tours. Open April–September, daily 10–5 (underground tours late May–late September, daily 10.30–5). Telephone: (01558) 650359.

construction of the Llyn Brianne Reservoir and a new through-road system northwards connecting with the Abergwesyn Pass to Tregaron in Mid Wales.

Despite its new role as a port of call on the way to Llyn Brianne, Rhandirmwyn has not changed much. The broad valley, flanked by green hills and bare mountains, is as beautiful as ever. The pleasant Royal Oak pub on the hillside in the middle of the village commands a fine view of these surroundings. Surprisingly, this placid country village owes its name and existence to an early industrial enterprise. Rhandirmwyn translates as 'lead mining area', a reference to the village's mining activity which spanned many hundreds of years (at one time, Rhandirmwyn boasted one of Europe's largest lead mines). By the 1930s, the last mine had closed. All that now remains are overgrown, abandoned levels in the hillsides and evidence of a washery and crushing plant hidden at the bottom of the valley.

From Rhandirmwyn ▲, continue on up the valley past Ystradffin, marked by a small church on the left of the road and, shortly after the church, the entrance and car park for the RSPB Dinas Hill reserve, also on your left. (This is the starting point for the walk which not only introduces you to the bird life of the area but takes you to the cave of Twn Shôn Cati – if you can find it!)

The little church has a fascinating history. Dedicated to St Paulinus, it stands on an ancient priests' trail established by the Cistercians in medieval times. When walking over the mountains to their abbey of Strata Florida at Pontrhydfendigaid, Mid Wales, the monks would stop off at Capella Sancti Paulinus, which they founded as a resting place in 1117. The church was restored in the nineteenth and twentieth centuries.

The white-robed Cistercian Order made a big impact on medieval Wales. Religion was not their only concern: from their abbeys, strung out all across Wales, they made a great contribution to Welsh life by improving the land, building bridges and laying roads. Most significantly, their expertise as farmers led to the successful establishment of sheap-rearing in Wales.

After visiting Dinas Hill, continue along the road

A tour of the Roman goldmines

northwards to the car park overlooking Llyn Brianne dam and reservoir. The reservoir, formed by collecting the headwaters of the Tywi and Camddwr rivers through the construction of a massive rock-filled dam – the highest in Britain – was opened in 1973. This huge 13,500 million-gallon lake supplies Swansea. Although not part of this tour, a spectacular 'new' road built at the same time as the reservoir runs along its eastern shores through silent, uninhabited high country to connect with the mountain road between Llanwrtyd Wells and Tregaron.

Return southwards from the dam, past the RSPB Visitor Centre. Two miles south-west of the RSPB Centre, turn right B (do not go all the way back to Rhandirmwyn) across the bridge over the river, then turn immediately right.

Follow this scenic road through remote farming country and the Cothi Valley to Pumsaint (on the A482). Just before joining the A482, stop off for a visit to the Roman Goldmines (National Trust) C.

Pumsaint itself is a small village scattered around the main road. Two thousand years ago, this peaceful community would have looked very different. A Roman camp, built to protect the mines, stood at the spot now occupied by the Dolaucothi Arms. The village is named after the legend of the Five Saints ('pump' in Welsh means 'five'). A misshapen rock at the entrance to the goldmines bears five indentations, said to be caused by the heads of five saints – Gwyn, Gwynno, Gwynnoro, Celynin and Ceitho – who passed this way whilst on pilgrimage to

the shrine of St David, patron saint of Wales. They supposedly used the stone as a communal pillow during a storm so fierce that it pressed their heads into the rock, leaving permanent evidence of its force. There is a more believable, if boring explanation. The stone, according to some, was used to pound ore from the mines.

After visiting the Roman Goldmines, turn left on to the A482 for Llanwrda.

A mile or so after the goldmines you will come to Felin Newydd Flour Mill, at the roadside on your left. This 200-year-old corn mill, one of Wales's few working watermills, still produces stoneground wholemeal flour in the traditional way.

At Llanwrda, turn left and follow the A40 along the Tywi Valley back to Llandovery. ■

CARMARTHEN, THE BRECHFA FOREST AND VALE OF TYWI

49 MILES – 2 ½ HOURS
START AND FINISH AT CARMARTHEN

This route gives an undiluted flavour of rural Wales. Starting at the country town of Carmarthen, a leading marketplace for South Wales's agricultural community, it travels into the hills, through farmlands and forests, before returning to the pastoral Vale of Tywi. On the way there are hidden villages, a picturesque ruined abbey, beautiful landscaped parklands and one of Wales's most romantic castles.

Leave Carmarthen on the A40 eastbound. On the eastern fringes of the town there is a large, sloping area on the northern side of the road (it is easily spotted, for there is a distinct break in the housing development). You can park the car and walk into its grassy bowl.

This is Carmarthen's Roman Amphitheatre, a little-known but significant historic site, one of only seven amphitheatres built in Britain.

A short distance further on, at Abergwili on Carmarthen's outskirts, call into Carmarthen Museum.

From Abergwili, the A40 runs above the looping River Tywi along the flank of a wide and verdant valley, one of South Wales's richest farming areas. In about a mile after the Abergwili, the wooded hill alongside the road is known as Merlin's Hill, named after the

---

• PLACES OF INTEREST •

Carmarthen
This attractive town, built on a rise above the River Tywi, is a prosperous administrative and market centre. There is an excellent food and produce market here on Wednesdays, the main market day, and Saturdays, as well as a thriving livestock mart. Carmarthen was the site of *Moridunum*, the westernmost Roman fort in Britain, and the town has legendary associations with Merlin the Magician. An ancient oak tree was removed during road improvements despite the prophecy 'When Merlin's Oak shall tumble down, then shall fall Carmarthen town'. The town's medieval heart, almost lost amongst modern development, is centred around the remnants of its castle – a gatehouse, parts of wall, keep and two towers. An impressive memorial west of the town centre celebrates a famous local hero General Sir Thomas

Picton, killed at the Battle of Waterloo in 1815. The Carmarthen Heritage Centre on the riverside traces the town back to its Roman origins, following nine different themes using the River Tywi as a link throughout. Open Easter–September daily 10–5, October–Easter daily 10–4. Telephone: (01267) 223788.

Carmarthen Museum
This is listed separately from Carmarthen because it is located at Abergwili, a mile or so from the

town centre. Housed in a magnificent building, a former Palace of the Bishops of St David's, it contains a wide range of folk items, Roman finds and military memorabilia. Local history, culture and the countryside are well represented, and upstairs there is a former chapel used by the bishops when in residence in their country retreat. Open 10–4.30. Telephone: (01267) 231691.

Talley Abbey
The abbey was founded in the twelfth century by the Welsh nobleman Rhys ap Gruffydd for the Premonstratensian Order. Its ruined central tower with its tall archway, set beside twin lakes, creates an evocative picture. Open summer daily 9.30–6.30, winter Monday–Saturday 9.30–4, Sunday 2–4. Telephone: (01558) 685444.

legendary Arthurian magician and topped by an Iron Age fort.

At Nantgaredig, turn left on to the B4310 for Brechfa and Abergorlech.

North of the Tywi, the landscape changes quite dramatically within a few miles. The road winds its way past the tongue-twisting hamlets of Felingwmisaf and Felingwmuchaf into deepest South Wales, a rolling countryside of enclosed little valleys and hill sheep farmlands. The village of Brechfa, in the foothills of Mynydd Llanybydder, gives its name to the Brechfa Forest, a huge conifer plantation which covers much of the wild upland to the north.

Go straight on at Brechfa, still following the B4310. The road between Brechfa and Abergorlech follows the tranquil River Cothi through an off-the-beaten-track valley frequented mainly by fishermen in search of *sewin* (sea-trout) and salmon. For walkers, Abergorlech is the starting-point for a number of waymarked forest trails. The walks start from the car park in the village.

Talley's lakeside Abbey

At Llansawel, take the B4337 south-eastwards, turning right in 1½ miles on to the B4302 for Talley. In Talley, just after the Edwinsford Arms, turn right A off the B4302 for Talley Abbey and lake.

The remote village of Talley enjoys an idyllic setting beside two lakes surrounded by silent hills. Take a look into St Michael's, an unusual church dating from the late eighteenth century which – with its box pews and lack of central aisle – looks more like a traditional Welsh chapel. If the weather is fine, the lakeside ruins of Talley Abbey (about the halfway point of the route) are a perfect

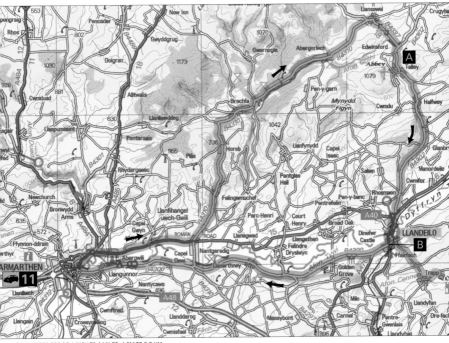

SCALE 1:250 000 OR 1 INCH TO 4 MILES *1 CM TO 2.5 KM*

55

spot for a picnic lunch. **After visiting the abbey, rejoin the B4302 southwards through more peaceful farming country, turning right at the A40 on the outskirts of Llandeilo.**

Back in the Vale of Tywi, Llandeilo is a pleasant country town with an attractive range of inns and shops. **Leave Llandeilo by the A483 southwards.**

Llandeilo, on a hill beside the Tywi

Cross the bridge (reputedly the longest single-span stone bridge in Wales), and just over the river at Ffairfach turn left for a detour of a few miles along the minor road (signposted) to Carreg Cennen Castle (Cadw-Welsh Historic Monuments) at Trapp, a few miles away. Park in the official castle car park and walk up through the farm, where

you purchase your admission ticket. **After visiting the castle, return to this junction at Ffairfach and go straight across the A483 on to the A476. Just over ½ mile after Ffairfach, turn right off the A476 on to the B4300.**

This 'B' road follows the southern side of the Vale of Tywi. It is a quiet, mainly straight route (most of the heavy traffic uses the A40 which runs parallel to it on the other side of the river), so you will have the opportunity to savour this lovely valley.

In 2 miles, turn left on to the minor road for a short detour, following the signs for Gelli Aur Country Park. After visiting the park, rejoin the B4300 which leads directly back to Carmarthen.

On the way back to Carmarthen you will pass close to two sites of note. About 2 miles after Gelli Aur, the B4297 to your right leads directly across the wide valley. By the bridge over the River Tywi it passes beneath the ruins of Dryslwyn Castle (Cadw-Welsh Historic Monuments). Scant remnants of this once-important site are scattered across the summit of a steep hill, all that is left of a medieval stronghold which once guarded the vale.

Llandeilo

Like Carmarthen, Llandeilo is set on a hill above the Vale of Tywi. It is a busy little town serving the local farming community, with a livestock market every other Monday. There is an attractive walk through the Castle Woods Nature Reserve, a 62-acre (25-hectare) sanctuary based around wooded cliffs to the west of the town. The reserve fringes Dinefwr Park, a handsome expanse of parkland landscaped by Capability Brown between 1775 and 1778, and home to herds of White Park cattle and fallow deer. It contains two historic sites – the medieval ruin of Dinefwr Castle, home of the powerful 'Lord Rhys', Rhys ap Gruffydd, and the Victorian-Gothic mansion (partly open) of Newton House. The great stately home of Newton House, dating from the seventeenth century, is currently under restoration, though parts of the interior are open to the public. Dating from the seventeenth century, it was remodelled in the 1850s in the then-fashionable baronial style. Mansion and park are in the care of the National Trust. Open (mansion and park) April–October, daily 10.30–5 (Library and Drawing Room may be closed to the public on Wednesdays, though not in July and August). Park open throughout winter in daylight hours. Telephone: (01558) 823902.

Carreg Cennen Castle, Trapp

Without doubt one of the most spectacular castles in Wales, Carreg Cennen is perched on a precipitous crag. Any attack on this 'eagles's nest' of a castle must have presented a formidable challenge. Today's visitors follow a path through a traditional Welsh farmyard which leads up a steep, grassy hillside to the heavily defended gateway. Nature, in the form of a sheer cliff, does the defending work on the other side of the castle. The views from the top of this atmospheric, weatherbeaten ruin are superb. To the south are the desolate moors of the Black Mountain, the wildest, most challenging highland terrain in the Brecon Beacons National Park. On a clear day, you can see northwards all the way to the mountains of Mid Wales. This memorable castle even has its own underground cavern, accessible by a spectacular passageway cut into the cliff face. During excavations, the skeletons of four prehistoric inhabitants were found here. Open summer daily 9.30–6.30 (until 8 in high summer), winter Monday–Saturday 9.30–4, Sunday 9.30–4. Telephone: (01558) 822291.

Gelli Aur Country Park

The park is ranged around a magnificent mansion, once the country seat of the Vaughan and Cawdor families. Gelli Aur (the 'Golden Grove') is a lovely 90-acre (36-hectare) country park set on a wooded hillside above the Vale of Tywi. Its features include an arboretum and terrace garden, nature trails, deer park, picnic areas and a visitor centre (there is restricted access to the mansion). Open April–September, daily 10–7, October–March, daily 10–5. Telephone: (01558) 668885.

Access is free and unrestricted.

A little further along the B4300, on the horizon to the south, you will see the stark outline of a single tower. This is Paxton's Tower (National Trust), an early nineteenth-century folly built by prominent local figure Sir William Paxton in honour of Lord Nelson.

Return along the B4300 to Carmarthen. ∎

Gelli Aur Country Park

CARMARTHENSHIRE COUNTRYSIDE AND COASTLINE

46 MILES – 2 ½ HOURS
START AND FINISH AT LLANELLI

This part of Wales is an unusual mixture of rural and industrial. In the nineteenth century, Llanelli and Kidwelly were major tinplate manufacturing centres. The area, in the far west of the South Wales coalfield, also saw mining activity for high-quality anthracite coal. Bygone times are remembered at Kidwelly's industrial museum. Elsewhere, you have to look long and hard for evidence of the heavy industries of old. Most of the tour concentrates on rural Carmarthenshire, a green and productive farming area where hills roll down to peaceful estuaries and the sandy coastline of Carmarthen Bay.

Wildfowl and Wetlands Centre

Llanelli's spirit of enterprise has in recent years found expression in new ways. On the face of it, Llanelli is a dyed-in-the-wool South Wales town: it is proud of its past as an important tinplate manufacturing centre and is utterly devoted to its rugby (the 'Scarlets' are a top club rugby team, and the rousing local anthem sung throughout Wales, *Sospan Fach* ('The Little Saucepan') harks back to a staple industrial product – there are even saucepans on top of the rugby posts in Llanelli's hallowed Stradey Park!).

Yet changes are afoot. The town has capitalised on its location on the Loughor Estuary, an area rich in birdlife, by establishing a Slimbridge-style Wildfowl and Wetlands Centre. And it has lately been successful

The verdant Vale of Tywi

in a bid to the Millennium Commission, attracting a 50 per cent grant for the far-reaching £30 million Llanelli Coastal Park waterfront redevelopment.

From the town centre, take the A476 north towards Tumble and Cross Hands. In just over 2 miles from the town centre, turn left **A** off the A476 on to a minor road for a short detour to the Lliedi reservoirs. (NB. This turning is unsignposted with no distinguishing features – it is the first left-hand turn you come to after leaving Llanelli's northern urban developments.) It brings you to the narrow neck of land between the upper and lower reservoirs, where you can park your car. There is also another turning left before the one described: this turn-off brings you to the foot of the lower reservoir.

The two reservoirs, set in a wooded valley, are a picture of tranquillity. Their sense of seclusion is heightened by the mature mixed woodlands which enclose their shores. The lower reservoir, in an area known locally as 'Swiss Valley', forms the focal point of a pleasant country park where you can follow a scenic footpath, about 2 miles long, which runs around the entire lake. The reservoir's

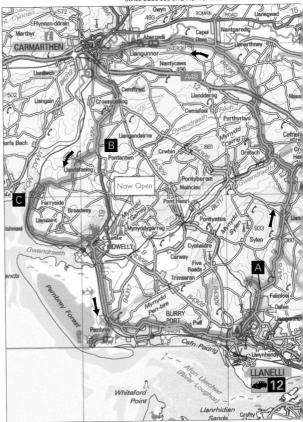

peacefulness attracts a variety of waterfowl, including moorhen, coot, heron and great crested grebe.

After visiting the reservoirs, rejoin the A476 northwards. At Tumble, take the B4317/B4310 through Drefach to Porthyrhyd, staying on the B4310 until its junction with the B4300, where you turn left for

---

• PLACES OF INTEREST •

Llanelli

Llanelli is a bustling town with good shopping, a covered market and pleasant parklands. The People's Park, located behind the decorative, neo-Jacobean town hall, is just a short walk from the pedestrianised shopping centre. Parc Howard, on the hill above, is a particularly fine park with superb rose gardens. Parc Howard's Mansion House, the former home of the tinplate magnate Lord Stepney, is now a museum housing an extensive collection of rare and collectable items of Llanelli pottery as well as

exhibits tracing the history of the local tinplate industry. Museum open Easter– September, Monday–Friday 11–1, 2–6, Saturday and Sunday 2–6; October–Easter, Monday–Friday 11–1, 2–4, Saturday and Sunday 2–4. Telephone: (01554) 772029.

The Wildlife and Wetlands Centre is based along a stretch of the wide estuary of sand and saltmarsh where the River Loughor meets the sea, one of the most important wetland sites in Wales. The 200-acre (81-hectare) reserve has wildfowl from all over the world, including Australian

magpie geese, hottentot teal from Africa, multi-coloured mandarins from China and flamingos. At high tide, thousands of birds fly in with the advancing waters. The reserve has a lake, observation points, walkways, wonderful views across the estuary and a visitor centre where activities for children include wildlife brass rubbings and badge-making. Open summer daily 9.30–5, winter daily 9.30–4. Telephone: (01554) 741087.

Carmarthen

Please see description in Tour 11.

Kidwelly

This ancient town received its first charter under Henry I. Kidwelly Castle, with its soaring twin-towered, three-storeyed gatehouse, is one of the best preserved in Wales and an outstanding example of the concentric 'walls within walls' system of thirteenth-century defence. Developed over the course of more than three centuries of Anglo-Welsh conflict, Kidwelly's half-moon shape stems from a twelfth-century stockaded Norman fortress defended on one side by the Gwendraeth Fâch River and on the other by a deep, crescent-shaped ditch. The castle has been the setting for many films and dramas as a result of its impressive location and well-preserved battlements. Open summer daily 9.30–6.30, winter Monday–Saturday 9.30–4, Sunday 11–4. Telephone: (01554) 890104.

Fragments of the fortified medieval town which grew up around the castle survive amongst Kidwelly's streets. The south gateway, the main entrance to the castle precinct, dates from the thirteenth century, as does the Church of St Mary, with its fine tower and spire, built to serve a nearby Benedictine priory. Just south-west of the town, on the mouth of the Gwendraeth Fach, is Kidwelly Old Quay. The saltings and low-tide mudflats of a harbour that thrived during Kidwelly's days as a trading port provide fine views over the Gwendraeth Estuary. Now renovated, the quay has boating facilities, picnic areas and walkways.

On the north-eastern outskirts of the town is the Kidwelly Industrial Museum, set on the banks of the Gwendraeth Fâch River and based on the remnants of the Kidwelly Tinplate Works which operated from 1737 until 1941. The museum is unique in that it is the only one in Britain where tinplate machinery is on display at its original working site. An exhibition illustrates what tin plate is, how it is made, and the various uses to which it is put. On site are the hot rolling mill and cold rolls where metal plates were finished before being tinned. The industrial museum also includes a coal museum based on pit head gear, a winding engine, and diesel and steam locomotives, all illustrating the progress of mechanisation during the Industrial Revolution. Open Easter– October, Monday–Friday 10–5, Saturday and Sunday 2–5. Telephone: (01554) 891078.

Pembrey Country Park

Pembrey is a 500-acre (202-hectare) park that includes an unconventional mix of beech, conifer forest and grassland. The park is fronted by Cefn Sidan, a magnificent 7-mile stretch of gently sloping sand that has been described as one of Europe's best beaches. Fringed by dunes and with views from the Gower Peninsula west to Pembrokeshire, the beach is also noted for its swimming and fishing. There is a wide variety of activities and attractions in this popular park, including forest walks, nature trails, pitch and putt, a narrow-gauge railway, dry ski slope and toboggan run, falconry centre and equestrian centre. For full details, go first to the park's visitor centre. The park is open all year, its main attractions from June to August, daily. Telephone: (01554) 833913.

Carmarthen.

The 'B' road runs along the southern flank of the lovely Vale of Tywi, a rich farming area set amongst green, rolling hills. **At the roundabout on the southern approach to Carmarthen (by the railway station), take the A484 southwards for Kidwelly.** If you want to visit Carmarthen (featured on Tour 11), you should take a short detour northwards here for the town centre.

About 2 ½ miles after Cwmffrwd, turn right B off the A484 on to the minor road for Ferryside. Ferryside, perched on the banks of the beautiful Tywi Estuary, is a charming spot. Although the railway line to south-west Wales passes through as it hugs the coast to Carmarthen, the main road steers well clear, giving Ferryside a forgotten air. In its time, it has been an understated little seaside resort and a cockle-picking centre, vestiges of which still remain along with its modern role as a modest sailing centre.

These evocative surroundings, close to the confluence of three rivers – the Tywi, Tâf and

Looking across the estuary from Ferryside to Llansteffan

Kidwelly's well-preserved castle

Gwendraeth – as they mingle with themselves and the waters of Carmarthen Bay, inspired writer and poet Dylan Thomas who lived at Laugharne a few miles to the west (see Tour 13). Directly opposite Ferryside on the opposite bank of the Tywi is Llansteffan, a village of white cottages nestling beneath a ruined headland castle dating from medieval times.

After Ferryside, stay on the coast road C, which skirts the Tywi and Gwendraeth estuaries, for Kidwelly. Just after Ferryside, this wonderfully scenic road clings to a hill with an even better view – Tregoning Hill, a National Trust property accessible by a short footpath. Beneath the hill to the south is the roadside St Ishmael's Church. This little church, with its crooked window, buttresses and sundial set above its entrance, is as old as it looks. The rocky area below, revealed at low tide, is the site of the lost village of Hawton, destroyed in a severe storm hundreds of years ago.

Continue along the coast road, which now follows the Gwendraeth Estuary, to Kidwelly. This marshy estuary is noted for its dune formations and rare plant life including fen orchids and Welsh gentians, both of national significance.

After visiting Kidwelly Castle (Cadw-Welsh Historic Monuments) in the centre of town and the Kidwelly Industrial Museum (located at the old tinplate works on the north-eastern approaches to the town), rejoin the A484 for Pembrey and Llanelli. The road runs along a flat coastal plain fronted by the vast sweep of Cefn Sidan Sands, one of the longest beaches in Wales. Before reaching Pembrey, you will see on your right the entrance to the Welsh Motor Sports Centre, an up-and-coming racetrack which holds a full and varied programme of events and is used by many Formula One teams for testing.

At Pembrey, take a short detour south to the Pembrey Country Park before returning to Llanelli via Burry Port. ∎

Pembrey Country Park

• TOUR 13 •

WESTWARDS ALONG CARMARTHEN BAY

49 MILES – 2½ HOURS
START AND FINISH AT CARMARTHEN

This tour follows the sandy western arc of Carmarthen Bay to Amroth and Saundersfoot at the gateway to the Pembrokeshire Coast National Park. Those familiar with the works of poet and writer Dylan Thomas will know that this part of Wales held a special magic for him. He lived for some years at Laugharne, where his Boathouse home is now a museum dedicated to his memory. The seemingly endless sands beyond Laugharne curl around to Saundersfoot, a popular resort and sailing centre. Places to visit just inland from the coast include a delightful National Trust garden and an attractive crafts village where you can see craftspeople at work.

Leave Carmarthen by the A40 westbound. The fast dual-carriageway road shortly brings you to St Clears, where you take the A4086 for Laugharne and Pendine.

In the 1840s, St Clears was a focus for the Rebecca Riots, an uprising against toll roads in which rioters dressed in female garb. After St Clears, you enter quintessential 'Dylan Thomas Country', the timeless landscapes and seascapes that inspired so much of his work. Sleepy Laugharne, on the Tâf Estuary, is the sea-town where he spent some of the happiest and most productive years of his life.

Laugharne lies at the eastern end of Pendine Sands. This huge 6-mile beach mirrors Cefn Sidan Sands across Carmarthen Bay (see Tour 12). After Laugharne, you will not get a glimpse of the sands until you come to Pendine itself, a small seaside centre completely dwarfed by its massive beach. Pendine Sands were used for land-speed record attempts in the 1920s, witnessing the epic battle between Sir Malcolm Campbell in *Blue Bird* and Welsh driver J G Parry-Thomas in *Babs*. It ended in tragedy in 1927 when

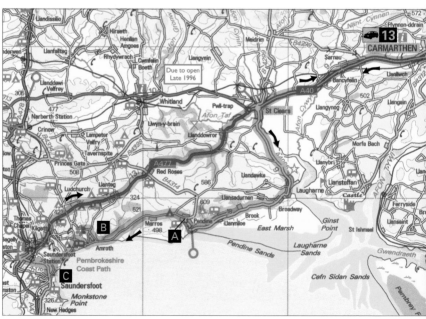

SCALE 1:250 000 OR 1 INCH TO 4 MILES *1 CM TO 2.5 KM*

Laugharne Castle

also witnessed another record-breaking attempt when Amy Johnson took off from here in 1933 on her flight across the Atlantic.

Leave Pendine on the B4314 and take the minor road west to Amroth. At Amroth, you enter the Pembrokeshire Coast National Park, Britain's only coastal-based national park. From here, the park's boundary stretches almost unbroken all the way around the tip of south-west Wales to Poppit Sands near Cardigan, a distance of about 180 miles. Amroth is also the start of the long-distance Pembrokeshire Coast Path.

Amroth itself is a quiet little seaside village, with plenty of seafront parking next to an attractive beach of gently shelving sands. So gently do the sands shelve that they create shallow water which – according to the locals at least! – are warmer than anywhere else along this coast. At

Parry-Thomas was killed while trying to beat the record of 174.88 mph set by Campbell. For many years, the wrecked *Babs* lay buried beneath the sands. In 1971 it was dug up by an enthusiast and has now been fully restored. There are mementoes of the heroic land-speed days at Pendine's seafront hotel. Pembrey

---

• PLACES OF INTEREST •

Carmarthen
Please see description in Tour 11.

Laugharne
Untroubled Laugharne, located away from it all on the mouth of the lovely Tâf Estuary, is a stranger to the rush of modern times. Dylan Thomas said that he 'got off the bus and forgot to get on again' when he came to Laugharne, and the town is perhaps best known for its connections with Wales's much-loved poet. He lived here with his wife Caitlin and their three children from 1949 until his untimely death on an American lecture tour in 1953. Laugharne was one of the main sources of inspiration for his most famous work, *Under Milk Wood*, a mesmeric 'play for voices' set in the fictitious sea-town of Llareggub (read it backwards!).

Dylan wrote in a little shack along the lane from his home at The Boathouse, an idyllically located house perched on the

estuary's 'heron-priested shore'. From the town centre, The Boathouse, now a museum dedicated to the poet's life and work, is accessible via the narrow Cliff Road from the town centre. Downstairs in the family living room Dylan's voice can be heard, emanating from a period wireless set, reading his own works. The upper floor houses a gallery of local artists' paintings. Open Easter–October, daily 10–6, November–Easter, daily 10.30–3.30. Telephone: (01994) 427420.

Dylan's writing shed can be

seen along the lane, looking as if the poet has just popped out for a drink at Brown's Hotel in Laugharne's main street, where he was a regular customer. Following Dylan's death in New York, his body was brought back to Laugharne for burial in St Martin's churchyard. His grave is marked by a simple white cross.

The town's history is also strongly linked with its castle (Cadw-Welsh Historic Monuments), which dates from the thirteenth century. In Tudor times Sir John Perrot – who also played a large part in the remodelling of Carew Castle (see Tour 15) – converted the castle into a fine gentleman's residence. The remains, picturesquely situated along the estuary, have been extensively restored and a Victorian plant garden has been recreated within the grounds. Opening times to be confirmed. Please ring (01222) 500242/500261 for more details.

low tide, the stumps of an ancient submerged forest can be seen.

At Amroth, take a short detour **B** to the National Trust's Colby Woodland

Garden (signposted off the coast road). After Amroth, stay on the minor road south-westwards through Wiseman's Bridge for Saundersfoot.

During World War II, the small, steep beach at Wiseman's Bridge was the scene of a rehearsal for the Normandy D-Day landings, watched over by Winston

• PLACES OF INTEREST •

Colby Woodland Garden, Amroth
This National Trust garden is set in a wooded, steep-sided valley stretching inland from Amroth. It is part of the Trust's 973-acre (394-hectare) Colby Estate which comprises woodlands, farmlands and a ¾-mile stretch of coast between Amroth and Wiseman's Bridge. The estate centres on Colby Lodge, a three-storey house built in 1803–5 for the Colby family of Ffonnonau, north Pembrokeshire, under the supervision of a pupil of George Nash. The house is privately occupied, but its secluded, beautiful 8-acre (3-hectare) grounds and gardens are open to the public.

There are miles of woodland paths, some leading to high viewpoints with breathtaking vistas of the coast. The woodland garden is best seen from mid-April when the daffodils are in blossom, followed in May and June by the rich hues of the rhododendrons and azaleas. The sheltered and

immaculately maintained walled garden, once a kitchen garden, is now full of choice herbaceous plants and shrubs. It also contains an elegant Gothic-style gazebo with a trompe l'oeil painting. Open April– October daily 10–5 (walled garden 11–5). Telephone: (01834) 811885.

Saundersfoot
For an attractive seaside resort in a national park, Saundersfoot has a most unconventional history as a coal-exporting port. The harbour was built here in the 1820s to export the anthracite coal mined a short way inland and transported to the quay by railway (the remains of one of the old mines, the Grove Colliery, and nineteenth-century ironworks can be seen in the woods to the south of Stepaside). The coal trade ceased at the start of World War II. Today, Saundersfoot is a favoured port of call with sailing and watersports enthusiasts. There are good beaches either side of the harbour, while to the north, between

Saundersfoot and Wiseman's Bridge, are the pretty sands of Coppet Hall. South from the resort you can follow the Pembrokeshire Coast Path around the headland of Monkstone Point to neighbouring Tenby (see Tour 15), a few miles away.

Stepaside Craft Village
This craft village and workshops, the only one of its kind in Pembrokeshire, brings together a range of different skills. The village consists of individual craft cabins situated in woodland surroundings. Craftspeople in residence include a gold and silver jeweller, woodturner, leatherworker, painter and textile artist. Visitors can usually see the craftsperson at work as well as purchase items. Other facilities here include picnic sites, tea room and woodland walks. Open April–October, Monday–Friday 10–5, Sunday 11–5. Telephone: (01834) 811686.

Churchill. From Wiseman's Bridge, you can follow walks inland along the wooded Pleasant Valley towards Stepaside.

Saundersfoot, which has grown up around its harbour, is one of Pembrokeshire's most popular spots. The resort boasts a large sheltered beach, plentiful accommodation and the predictable range of seaside amusements, though the latter are – for once – not too intrusive.

From Saundersfoot, take the B4316 C north. Turn right on to the A478. In just over ½ mile you will come to a large roundabout on the approach to Kilgetty. If you wish, you can take a short detour north along the A478 from here to Folly Farm, an entertaining family tourist attraction – a great favourite with children – based at a large working dairy farm with the usual displays of animals, farm machinery and so on. (Beside the roundabout itself there is a large Tourist Information Centre, well stocked with information on Pembrokeshire.) **Otherwise, from the roundabout take the A477 back to St Clears, within a mile turning off for the Stepaside Craft Village.**

Follow the brown road signs to the village of Stepaside, and you will find the car park on Pleasant Valley.

After visiting Stepaside, return to the A477 eastbound through Red Roses to St Clears. Just before reaching St Clears you will drive through the village of Llanddowror, significant as the home of Griffith Jones (1684–1761), a great religious leader and pioneer educationalist who organised travelling schools in which people were taught to read.

At St Clears, rejoin the A40 for Carmarthen. ■

Amroth, at the gateway to the Pembrokeshire Coast National Park

THE TEIFI VALLEY

34 MILES (68 MILES ROUND TRIP) –
2 HOURS (4 HOURS ROUND TRIP)
START AT CARDIGAN, FINISH AT LAMPETER

This is one of only two linear tours in the book. Geography dictates the route, for it follows the Teifi Valley from Cardigan eastwards into the hills at Lampeter. This valley is one of the loveliest in Wales. The Teifi charts a course between low hills and green farmlands, an off-the-beaten-track landscape dotted with traditional country towns and villages. This valley was not always so peaceful. In the latter part of the nineteenth century, it was Wales's busiest wool-producing area. Memories of those times are recalled at a fascinating museum en route.

Cardigan, on the mouth of the River Teifi, is an historic market town. Today, it successfully combines the twin roles of country town and well-located holiday centre on the doorstep of Pembrokeshire's north coast and

---

• PLACES OF INTEREST •

Cardigan

The old county town of Cardiganshire, historic Cardigan is strategically sited at the mouth of the River Teifi. Today Cardigan is a busy holiday centre on the doorstep of some of South Wales's loveliest countryside and coastline. It also continues to be a busy market town, with a twice-weekly general market (Monday and Saturday) and a livestock mart every Monday. The town's covered market is set up around the arcades of the Guildhall, an architecturally impressive building dating from the mid-nineteenth century.

Ruined Cardigan Castle has a complex history and has experienced at least one change of location. As we now see it, the castle occupies a high bluff overlooking the River Teifi. The stronghold was fortified in stone by Rhys ap Gruffydd, the influential

Welsh ruler, in the 1170s. In 1250, a new keep and town walls were added, at which point Edward I, the English king, based a local seat of administration here. The castle, like many others, was eventually destroyed by Cromwell – what remains today is in private ownership.

Below the castle, a centuries-old multi-arched stone bridge spans the Teifi. These waters were once navigated by large craft when Cardigan was a thriving port – Wales's second most important – and a busy shipbuilding centre. Warehouses lining the waterfront are reminders of those times, while in the town itself, many inns date back to the days of the stagecoach.

The town has a revered place in Welsh history as the location of the first eisteddfod, held at Cardigan Castle under the patronage of Lord Rhys in 1176. In 1976, the Royal

National Eisteddfod – Wales's largest and most important cultural festival – returned to the town to commemorate the 800th anniversary of the original event.

National Coracle Centre and Cenarth Mill

The National Coracle Centre houses a unique collection of coracles from all over the world, including examples from India, Iraq, North America, Vietnam and, of course, Wales. The centre also has demonstrations of the ancient art of coracle making. Open Easter–October, Sunday–Friday 10.30–5.30. Telephone: (01239) 710980/710209.

The centre stands in the grounds of a seventeenth-century flour mill which is also open to the public and offers rural crafts, gifts and works of art for sale. Both the coracle centre and mill are located near the cascading Cenarth Falls.

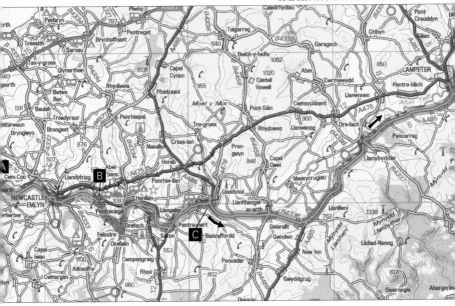

the coves and headlands of Cardigan Bay. The town is by-passed by the A487 coast road.

The A484 along the Teifi Valley to Newcastle Emlyn meets the by-pass at a roundabout just east of the town centre. Follow this road to Llechryd. Llechryd is the first of the string of pretty riverside villages you will come across in this beautiful valley. The Teifi Valley is rich in tradition. The medieval traveller and chronicler, Giraldus Cambrensis ('Gerald of Wales'), singled out the Teifi as the finest salmon river in Wales.

This river is famous not only for its salmon and sea-trout (known locally as *sewin*) but also for the method by which the fish are caught. You can still see coracles working on the Teifi, especially on the stretch between Cilgerran (just west of Llechryd) and Cenarth. The coracle, a tiny one-man boat, has been used in Wales for over 2,000 years. When Giraldus Cambrensis saw them in the twelfth century, they were already regarded as ancient craft. The boat, which resembles an upturned umbrella, is made of intertwined laths of willow and hazel with a waterproof skin coated in a layer of black pitch.

The boats are extremely light and, in practised hands, very manoeuvrable. The coracle fishermen usually work in pairs with a net drawn across the salmon run.

After Llechryd, the A484 runs beside the Teifi as it snakes along a wooded riverbank, crossing the river

at Cenarth **A**. This village was one of Wales's earliest tourist attractions. No Victorian Grand Tour of Wales was complete without a visit to the falls in Cenarth, where the Teifi tumbles over rocks before rushing beneath a picturesque old stone bridge. Salmon leap up the falls, 'as high as the tallest spear'

The Teifi meets the sea at Cardigan Bay

Coracles at Llechryd

according to Giraldus. Stop off here to admire the view and to visit the National Coracle Centre and Cenarth Mill. In summer, coracle races are held here.

From Cenarth, it is only a short drive to the market town of Newcastle Emlyn. Apart from market day on Friday, you will not have trouble finding a parking place in this characterful old town, located on a loop on the Teifi. Nowadays, its castle hardly lives up to its name. The thirteenth-century ruins, consisting of parts of the gatehouse and walls, make the

most of the natural defences afforded by the river on three sides. The town itself has a scattering of interesting buildings. Look out for the Victorian Town Hall and Bethel Chapel (near the church), a good example of nineteenth-century Welsh chapel architecture.

In less than 2 miles after Newcastle Emlyn turn right B off the A484 at Pentrecagal for the Museum of the Welsh Woollen Industry (signposted). Within 1 ½ miles, turn sharp left at the church in Felindre for the

museum (again signposted). The museum is located shortly on the left.

The Teifi Valley was also famous for its woollen mills, which took advantage of the soft, clear-flowing waters to wash the wool and drive the weaving machines by waterwheel. The now-peaceful riverbanks once echoed to the clatter of many mills, so much so that there was 'hardly a spot on the bank ... where it would be convenient to build an additional factory or mill'. By the late nineteenth century there were no less than 52 mills in full production here, manufacturing mainly flannel cloth for industrial South Wales. But the boom was short-lived, for there was a catastrophic decline in the 1920s. The handful of mills which still survive now tend to specialise in the distinctive Welsh cloth woven in patterns based on Celtic designs.

After visiting the museum, proceed northwards along the minor road from Drefach for just over ½ mile, turning right at the A484. In another ½ mile, turn left on to the B4335 which brings you to

Cenarth Falls

Pentre-cwrt and the A486, where you turn left for Llandysul. (NB: If you want to ride on the narrow-gauge Teifi Valley Railway, take the following very short detour. Instead of turning right on to the A484 after Drefach, go straight across for Henllan on the northern side of the river. You will shortly come to the railway terminus.)

On the approach to Llandysul, turn right off the A486 on to the B4336 **C** just before the bridge (to visit Llandysul itself stay on the 'A' road, then retrace your steps). Llandysul, built in a series of terraces on a hillside above the Teifi, is another former woollen town. At its base stands the imposing Church of St Tysul, dating from the thirteenth century, with a large castellated tower and fine Early English interior. A few centuries ago the church porch served as one of the goals in a long-distance football match played on every New Year's Day between Llandysul and Llanwenog, 5 miles away! Sporting activities nowadays are confined to fishing and canoeing along a challenging white-water stretch of the Teifi as it rushes through a narrow course by the road bridge to the south of the church. A weekly livestock market is held here each Tuesday.

The B4336 from Llandysul will bring you to the A485, where you turn left for Llanybydder. This obscure little country town enjoys great fame in equine circles as the location, on the last Thursday of each month, of a celebrated sale of horses. Said to be the biggest in Britain, the horse fair attracts buyers from far and wide, including overseas. Llanybydder's livestock market is held every other Monday.

Stay on the A485 after Llanybydder for a little more than 4 miles, turning left at the junction with the A482 for Lampeter, the tour's end, at the gateway to the upper Teifi Valley. ■

• PLACES OF INTEREST •

Museum of the Welsh Woollen Industry, Drefach-Felindre

The museum is located in the heart of what was once one of the busiest wool-producing areas in Wales, known for this reason as the 'Huddersfield of Wales'. Housed in the former Cambrian Mills, it contains an extensive collection of tools and machinery which demonstrates the industry's technical history. A working interpretative exhibition illustrates the production of woollen cloth from fleece to fabric, and there is also a fully working mill, Melin Teifi, on site, geared towards modern production. Within the museum grounds there are a number of craft workshops. Open April–September, Monday–Saturday 10–5, October–March, Monday–Friday 10–5. Telephone: (01559) 370929.

Lampeter

Situated amongst a mixed landscape of rolling farmland and lonely, wild mountains, Lampeter is both a university and market town (its large livestock market is generally held on Tuesdays, alternating with Tregaron 11 miles to the north-east). The town, a pleasing mix of Georgian and Victorian architecture, has a long history as a meeting place for rural folk – in the eighteenth century, drovers would assemble here to gather sheep and cattle before the long drive over the hills to England's markets.

St David's University College is the smallest and oldest of the constituent colleges of the University of Wales. It was founded in 1822 by Bishop Burges, Bishop of St David's, so that Welsh students, prohibited by the expense of attending Oxford or Cambridge, could enjoy a university education. Opened in 1827, the neo-Gothic style college was modelled on the Oxbridge design. In 1965 it became part of the University of Wales and was greatly expanded. The college houses a notable collection of rare medieval manuscripts and first editions. A large earthen mound in the college grounds is all that remains of Lampeter's castle.

Llanybydder Horse Fair

TENBY AND
SOUTH PEMBROKESHIRE

22 MILES – 1 ½ HOURS
START AND FINISH AT TENBY

*South Pembrokeshire is sometimes known as the 'Little England beyond
Wales' because of the outside influences brought by centuries of
colonisation and sea-trading. Many place-names in south
Pembrokeshire are more Home Counties than Welsh, and Tenby
displays little of the ambience or architecture of a typical Welsh town.
The coastline on this tour is glorious. South Pembrokeshire's limestone
cliffs and sandy bays, protected as the Pembrokeshire Coast National
Park, are renowned for their natural beauty and wildlife. This tour also
has a deeply historical theme, calling in at some of Wales's most
impressive castles and the serene ruins of a bishop's palace.*

Tenby is Pembrokeshire's most popular resort. Yet unlike other seaside centres, this popularity has not brought with it the blight of over-commercialisation. In the nineteenth century, Tenby was described as 'the most celebrated of Welsh watering places … whose every view is picturesque in the extreme'. It is difficult to disagree with that judgement today when you stand on the Georgian harbour, or look out across the cliffs to large, uncluttered beaches, or wander the maze of medieval streets in the old town.

Remaining faithful to the past does pose problems, however, not least for the motor car. Tenby's narrow streets were not built for

Tenby's picturesque harbour

70

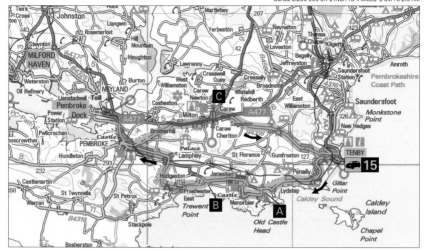

SCALE 1:250 000 OR 1 INCH TO 4 MILES *1 CM TO 2.5 KM*

modern traffic. In summer, car parking is difficult close to the seafront, though there are large parking areas within reasonable walking distance.

Take the A4139 westbound from Tenby towards Penally
and Lydstep. Penally, only a mile or so from Tenby, has access to the long, unbroken beach which sweeps back to the resort. The village was the site of an early Christian settlement, and is the reputed birth and burial place of
St Teilo. The wheel-cross at the church is an interesting monument, possibly dating from the ninth or tenth centuries, bearing a mixture of Celtic and Northumbrian decorative influences. The church also

---

• PLACES OF INTEREST •

Tenby
Almost every corner of Tenby has its charms. Pastel-shaded Georgian dwellings are stacked up like doll's houses along the old stone quayside. Hotels and guest houses line the cliffs above the beach. And the town is a maze of narrow passageways, enclosed within a ring of medieval walls.

Tenby's most famous historic feature is the Five Arches, the only surviving gateway of the three originally built to control entry to the town. There are, in fact, six arches in all, part of a round battlemented tower built into the medieval walls. The walls date from 1260, though they were strengthened and heightened in later centuries. To see them at their best walk along South Parade where they stand to their full height, incorporating two tiers of arrow-slits, a feature unique in Wales.

The well-preserved walls were designed to complement Tenby's medieval castle. Unfortunately, time has not been so kind to the old fortress, which lies in ruins on

the headland. Also on the headland is Tenby Museum, whose exhibits cover everything from art to natural history, maritime history to Tenby's long-standing role as a seaside resort.

Down below is the harbour, which has been a hive of activity for many centuries. Tenby's Welsh name is *Dinbych y Pysgod*, 'The Little Fort of the Fish'. The town's fishing ancestry is remembered at the harbourside 'Fisherman's Church' of St Justinian's Chapel. The original chapel, founded by the sea in 1539, was replaced by the existing one in 1878 'so once again the fisherfolk to the harbour church did go'.

Amongst the houses leading down to the harbour is the Tudor Merchant's House (National Trust), a fine three-storeyed dwelling which acts as a reminder of the days of Tenby's prosperous merchants and traders. It even boasts an indoor toilet, a luxurious feature indeed in the fifteenth and sixteenth centuries. Open April–September, Monday–Friday 10–5, Sunday 1–5, October,

Monday–Friday 10–3, Sunday 12–3. Telephone: (01834) 842279.

The only open space in medieval Tenby is occupied by the grand St Mary's Church, reputedly the largest parish church in Wales. Its steeple, soaring 152 feet (46 m) over the huddled rooftops, certainly looks the part. St Mary's stature can be explained by Tenby's prosperity as a thriving trading port, which funded a lavish rebuilding programme. The church's many monuments to prominent local merchants also reflect the maritime wealth of the town (there is a particularly good collection of these monuments in St Ann's Chapel).

Caldey Island, just offshore, is a beautiful and tranquil spot rich in wildlife and religious remains, including a medieval church and Cistercian abbey. The island is famous for its perfume, which is made by the monks of the abbey. In summer, there are regular boat trips from Tenby across to the island.

Manorbier Castle

Manorbier was the birthplace, in 1146, of Giraldus Cambrensis, better known perhaps as Gerald of Wales. In many ways, Giraldus was Wales's first travel writer. As a religious leader, he travelled extensively around Wales, recording his experiences for posterity. His castle has an idyllic location overlooking Manorbier's sandy bay. It is noted for the exceptional state of its preservation, both within and without, due to the durability of the local limestone from which it was built.

As with many Norman strongholds, the original castle here would have been built of wood and earth. The stone fortress, dating from the twelfth century, boasts many fine features including state apartments, a baronial hall and a powerful gatehouse. Open April–September, daily 10.30–5.30. Telephone: (01834) 871394.

Pembroke

Please see description in Tour 16.

Carew Castle

This handsome castle stands on the rivermeadows between the village and Tidal Mill. Carew

bridges the gap between the stark, purposeful military sites of earlier medieval times and the fortified manor houses of the later, more settled Middle Ages. The stronghold began life as a military fortification, plain and simple, built to take advantage of the seaborne access via the waters of the Milford Haven. Gradually it evolved into a graceful Tudor and Elizabethan home, displaying many fine features, decorative embellishments and creature comforts. Carew's mullioned windows – an unusual feature indeed for a Welsh castle – are particularly impressive. Much of the remodelling has been attributed to Sir John Perrot, reputedly the natural son of Henry VIII. Open April–October, daily 10–5. Telephone: (01646) 651782.

contains a memorial to those who died when the Caldey lifeboat capsized in 1843.

From Penally, the road hugs the coast to Lydstep. Just down from the village the sheltered, east-facing beach at Lydstep Haven tucks itself in between headlands (there is an attractive walk from the village to the limestone cliffs at Lydstep Point, the southern headland, with views eastwards across Caldey Sound to Caldey Island.

Just after Lydstep, leave the A4139 for the B4585 A, which loops around Manorbier before rejoining the 'A' road. Manorbier is a lovely spot, set amongst some of south Pembrokeshire's finest coastal scenery. According to medieval chronicler Giraldus Cambrensis ('Gerald of Wales'), Manorbier was 'the most delightful part of Pembroke... the pleasantest spot in Wales'. Although the accolade still rings true, it has to be recorded that he may have been a little biased: he was born at Manorbier Castle overlooking the sea.

Manorbier Bay has a delightful beach. If you are prepared to walk a mile or so in each direction there are other superb beaches to sample – Skrinkle Haven to the east and Swanlake Bay to the west.

Beach after beautiful beach presents itself on this tour. **One mile after Jameston, turn left B off the A4139 for the superb sands at Freshwater East, another sheltered east-facing beach (car parking can prove difficult here at the height of the season). From Freshwater East, return by the B4584 to the A4139 at**

The Pembrokeshire coast at Lydstep

Manorbier Castle

Lamphey. This small settlement, on the eastern approaches to Pembroke, is home to the splendid Lamphey Bishop's Palace (Cadw-Welsh Historic Monuments). In the fourteenth century, Lamphey was the favourite country residence for the bishops of St David's. The prelates of the medieval church lived in some style as country gentlemen, in comfortable, commodious dwellings set amongst orchards, fishponds and gardens. The shell of the Great Hall is most impressive, as is the attractive sixteenth-century chapel with a fine, five-light east window.

From Lamphey, stay on the A4139 for Pembroke, where you take the A4075/A477 eastbound (to visit the castle you will have to go into the centre of town). Pembroke is another town rich in history whose mighty castle ranks amongst the best in Wales. The town also boasts a remarkably well-preserved stretch of medieval town walls.

Just after Milton, turn left on to the A4075 for Carew. Quite apart from its pretty setting at the head of a tidal inlet which connects with the great Milford Haven Waterway, there are at least three reasons for stopping off at Carew. As you enter the village, on your left you will see an imposing wheel-head cross, 14 feet (4 m) tall, by the roadside. Its amazingly complicated interlacing motifs

and designs are unmistakeably Celtic. It dates from the eleventh century and bears an inscription commemorating Maredudd ap Edwin, King of Dyfed, who was killed in battle in 1035. One of the finest of its kind in Britain, it has been adopted by Cadw-Welsh Historic Monuments as its national symbol.

The effects of the tide can still occasionally be seen at the road bridge over the Carew River when the waters run perilously high, almost submerging the structure. The tides here have been harnessed to ingenious effect. A short walk downriver leads to Carew's Tidal Mill, the only one surviving in Wales and one of only three restored tidal mills in Britain. By damming the river, the four-storey corn mill trapped the tide, the waters of which then powered the mill wheel.

The third reason for visiting Carew is its magnificent castle (see Places of Interest).

Leave Carew by turning on to the minor road south-eastwards opposite Carew Cross C . In just over ½ mile, this road joins the A477 at Sageston. Turn left here, and within a short distance turn right on to the B4318 for Tenby.

This 'B' road takes you past the Manor House Wildlife and Leisure Park, a tourist attraction with something for all the family – birds, animals, falconry demonstrations, gardens, model railway exhibition and children's play areas – set in a 12-acre (5-hectare) wooded park. You can also take a short detour off the 'B' road for St Florence, a village noted for its unusual Flemish-inspired architectural influences (especially the chimneys) and thirteenth-century Church of St Florentius.

The B4318 then brings you back into Tenby. ∎

Lamphey Bishop's Palace

PEMBROKESHIRE'S SEA-CLIFFS

31 MILES – 2 HOURS
START AND FINISH AT PEMBROKE

This tour takes in Pembrokeshire at its finest – towering sea-cliffs, sandy bays, grassy headlands and teeming colonies of sea-birds. Ornithologists will have a field day amongst the cliffs at Stackpole Head and Stack Rocks, walkers can follow some of the best stretches of the long-distance Pembrokeshire Coast Path, and those interested in history can trace the route of the Tudor dynasty from its beginnings at Pembroke Castle.

The town of Pembroke, on a rise above the Pembroke River, grew up around its castle, first established here in the late eleventh century as a western outpost of Norman influence in Wales.

Leave Pembroke by the B4319 south to Stackpole and Bosherston. Turn left off the B4319 A on to the minor road for Bosherston.
Bosherston is a strange spot. The little village, with its Norman

cruciform church, is conventional enough. From the church you can walk to the man-made lily ponds of Bosherston Lakes, a trio of narrow lagoon-like inlets which weave their watery fingers inland through gently rolling countryside.

(NB: Bosherston Lakes can also be visited from the sandy cove of Broad Haven, accessible by minor road 1 mile south-east of Bosherston. You can follow a beautiful walk from Broad Haven beach eastwards along the Pembrokeshire Coast Path to Stackpole Head, a spectacular promontory with terrifyingly sudden drops to the sea. The cliffs here are a prolific breeding ground for sea-birds, especially guillemots, razorbills and kittiwakes. Continue a little further and you will come to Barafundle Bay, one of Pembrokeshire's prettiest beaches, and Stackpole Quay, reputedly the smallest harbour in Britain. The entire distance, there and back, is about 6 miles.)

After visiting Bosherston village and lakes, continue on the minor road south for 1 mile to the car park for St

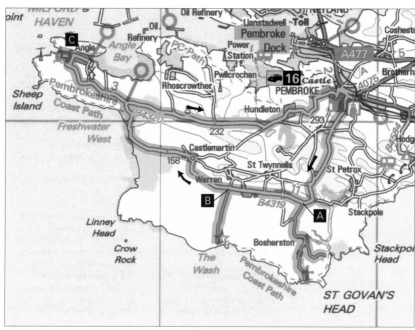

SCALE 1:166 666 OR ABOUT 1 INCH TO 2.5 MILES 1 CM TO 1.66 KM

The lily ponds at Bosherton

• PLACES OF INTEREST •

Pembroke

Pembroke, like Tenby, has a remarkable but little-known historical asset in the shape of its medieval town walls. The main street of the town occupies a long, high ridge above the river, a naturally strong defensive site further protected by a ring of fourteenth-century walls which, along the riverbank, are still virtually unbroken. Unlike Tenby, the main fortification here is in very good shape. Whereas Tenby's

castle is nothing but a ruin, Pembroke Castle stands tall and proud on a rocky bluff over the Pembroke River.

The castle was founded in around 1090, though as it stands today it dates from the later twelfth century and the arrival on the scene of the English knight William Marshall. Enter by the Great Gatehouse and you are confronted by the outer ward, a large grassy area lined with curtain walls and towers. The most famous of these is the so-called Henry VII Tower alongside the gateway. Harri Tudur, later to become Henry VII, first of the Tudors, was born at Pembroke Castle in 1457, reputedly in this tower (Harri's march from Pembrokeshire to victory at Bosworth Field over Richard III in 1485 is covered in Tour 17).

Dominating the inner ward is the castle's great round keep, a cylindrical tower almost 80 feet (24 m) high with buttressed walls

nearly 20 feet (6 m) thick and topped by an unusual stone dome. It is well worth climbing to the top for the view over the rooftops and river, from which you can appreciate Pembroke's natural and man-made defences to the full.

Pembroke's defences must have been up to the job. The medieval fortress was never captured by the Welsh. Moreover, it withstood a seven-week siege by Oliver Cromwell during the Civil War, only surrendering through lack of water. Open summer daily 9.30–6, winter daily 10–4. Telephone: (01646) 681510.

On Westgate Hill close to the castle is the Museum of the Home, an amazing place packed with over 3,000 exhibits spanning three centuries of home life. All human life is here, including cleaning, cooking, smoking and snuff-taking! Open May–September, Monday–Thursday 11–5. Telephone: (01646) 681200.

Beautiful Broad Haven

Govan's Head and St Govan's Chapel.

The chapel lies hidden at the base of the cliff. To the west, the coast path leads in about ½ mile to Huntsman's Leap, a strange sea fissure 130 feet (40 m) deep which slices through the headland. Legend has it that the huntsman who leapt across it on horseback died of shock! East of the chapel, the path runs along to St Govan's Head, another spectacular promontory.

From the car park at St Govan's, retrace your route through Bosherston back to the B4319, turning left. Turn left off the B4319 B 1 ½ miles before Castlemartin for Stack Rocks. (Please note: the road south to the coast crosses the Royal Armoured Corps Castlemartin Firing Range. When in use, as signified by red flags, this road is closed to the public.)

Stack Rocks deserve yet more superlatives. This pair of limestone pillars, cast adrift from the land by the erosive powers of the sea, stand straight out of the water. At 150 feet (45 m), Elegug Stack is the tallest; its sister, Elegug Spire, is about 20 feet (6 m) shorter. Bring your binoculars, for Stack Rocks support the largest colonies of sea-birds in Pembrokeshire that can be viewed from the mainland. The rich and varied birdlife here includes auks, fulmars, guillemots, kittiwakes and razorbills, the bird adopted as the symbol of the Pembrokeshire Coast National Park.

The relentless erosion caused by waves crashing on land has not progressed so far at the great sea arch which lies just to the west of Stack Rocks. The phenomenon, known as the Green Bridge of Wales, is an arch 80 feet (25 m) tall extending into the sea from the headland. Ultimately, it will collapse, leaving another sea-stack offshore.

After visiting Stack Rocks, return to the B4319, turning left, and drive through Castlemartin past the beach at Freshwater West, where Atlantic surf crashes

West Angle looks out across to Thorn Island

Bosherston Lakes

These lovely lakes are part of the National Trust's Stackpole Estate and the Stackpole National Nature Reserve. They were created in the late eighteenth century by damming the valley to provide a decorative feature for the grand, but now-demolished house of Stackpole Court. Three long lakes, joined at their base, stretch northwards through a landscape of fields and woodlands, a sheltered habitat favoured by a rich variety of birdlife including swans, mallard, kingfishers and heron.

But most people come to the lakes to see their waterlilies, which cover the surface and are at their best in June. The waterlilies thrive here because of the underlying limestone rock which creates non-acidic waters ideal for the plant. You can follow a circular lakeside path around the western lake for about 2 miles. From Bosherston, there is also access by foot along the lakes to the beach at Broad Haven and the coastal walk to Stackpole Head and Stackpole Quay (see details in the tour notes). The beach is separated from the lakes by a high bank of sand and shingle. The lakes, which cover 80 acres (32 hectares), are the largest expanse of open water in the Pembrokeshire Coast National Park.

St Govan's Chapel

This tiny chapel, which squeezes itself in amongst rocks at the base of a sea-cliff, is often quoted as one of the wonders of Wales. Probably dedicated to the Irish abbot Gobhan, a sixth-century contemporary of St David, it originally served as a hideaway for religious hermits. A staircase of worn stone steps leads down to the chapel, which as it now stands dates largely from the thirteenth

century. The well here, a place of pilgrimage until it dried up in the mid-nineteenth century, was said to cure eye troubles and crippled limbs.

Angle

Far-flung Angle has grown up around a long single street which connects two bays, West Angle at the mouth of Milford Haven and the sheltered waters of east-facing Angle Bay. In the days of coastal trading and fishing, Angle was a busy port. The village is more popular nowadays with holiday craft, though reminders of its nautical past survive in a tiny Seaman's Chapel with room for no more than 15 worshippers, founded in 1447, which stands behind St Mary's Church. Angle also has the remains of a medieval peel-tower.

The beautiful beach at West Angle Bay looks across the mouth of the Haven to St Anne's Head opposite. Just offshore is Thorn Island with its sturdy grey-stoned fort, one of many built in the nineteenth century to guard the Haven from the threat of French invasion. Bizarrely, the fort is now the ultimate away-from-it-all hotel.

---

dangerously on to the sands. Swimming is not recommended on this beach, though it is popular with surfers. **At the junction of the B4319 and B4320, turn left for Angle. Stay on the B4320 all the way into Angle, turning right C in the centre for the main body of the village and left for West Angle Bay.** Sleepy Angle is out on a limb, at the end of the road on a peninsula overlooking the mouth of the Milford Haven Waterway.

From Angle, return along the B4320 to Pembroke. On the way, you will see on your left a less appealing face of Pembrokeshire: unearthly petro-chemical installations lining the lower reaches of Milford Haven, taking advantage of the access which this deepwater inlet affords to massive supertankers.

Almost back in Pembroke, call in at Monkton Priory Church as you approach the town. This large church, on a hill opposite Pembroke Castle, is one of Pembrokeshire's most interesting religious buildings. Occupying the site of a medieval Benedictine priory founded in 1098, it has a fine Norman doorway and an interior noted for its unusually lofty and long vaulted plaster ceiling. The church was restored in the nineteenth century after many years of neglect. ■

A striking natural phenomenon – the Green Bridge of Wales

HAVERFORDWEST AND THE DALE PENINSULA

31 MILES – 2 HOURS
START AND FINISH AT HAVERFORDWEST

Haverfordwest is a bustling town, yet Pembrokeshire at its most remote is the dominant theme of this tour. The Dale Peninsula, in the far south-western corner of the Pembrokeshire Coast National Park, is tucked away on the road to nowhere. This is another tour which walkers will especially enjoy, for the coastal paths along Dale are some of the loveliest and quietest in Britain. Close by is another peninsula – Marloes – which boasts a magnificent beach. Little Haven and Broad Haven further up the coast are more traditional, and accessible, seaside holiday centres.

Haverfordwest, the old county town, is centrally located for visiting most of Pembrokeshire. The centre of the town is a maze of streets, some quite narrow, clustered around a steep hill crowned by a ruined castle. If you are approaching Haverfordwest along the A40 from the east, you will come to an efficient ring-road system which takes you around the town centre to pick up the B4327 for the Dale Peninsula.

Leave Haverfordwest by the B4327 to Dale. This 'B' road runs though flattish farmlands past scattered hamlets. It is an historic route, one used by Harri Tudur, the Welshman born at Pembroke Castle who became Henry VII, first of the Tudor monarchs. On 7 August 1485, Harri returned from exile in France, landing at Mill Bay on the Dale Peninsula. From there, he marched across Wales to the

Midlands, gathering forces on the way. On 22 August, he defeated Richard III at Bosworth Field to take the throne of England, thus inaugurating the mighty Tudor dynasty. As you drive along the B4327 about 2 miles north-east of Dale, you will cross an inconspicuous little stone bridge known as Mullock Bridge. Legend has it that the wily Welsh nobleman Sir Rhys ap Thomas lay under this bridge as Harri rode

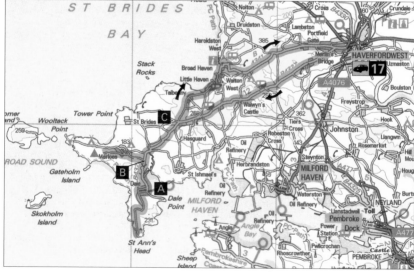

SCALE 1:250 000 OR 1 INCH TO 4 MILES *1 CM TO 2.5 KM*

Haverfordwest's ruined castle overlooks the town

over it, an act which preserved his integrity and his life, for he had promised King Richard that Harri would enter Wales 'only over his body'.

The B4327 runs into Dale along the placid waters of Dale Roads, a horseshoe-shaped landward-facing bay in the sheltered waters of the Milford Haven. Dale is a popular yachting and windsurfing centre with a shingle beach. It stands at the approach to an isolated, wildly beautiful peninsula, well off the beaten track, which has little difficulty in keeping itself to itself. Dale's safe anchorage has been appreciated by seamen for many centuries. Its name is Norse for 'valley' (Dale lies on a geological fault), a reflection of the strong Viking influence in this part of the world during the Dark Ages. A road leads south-eastwards from the village along the bay to Dale Point and Dale Fort, a nineteenth-century fortification built to defend the Haven's naval dockyards, which now serves as a field study centre.

From Dale, take the minor road southwards Ａ for 2½ miles along the peninsula to St Ann's Head. The road out of Dale runs westwards for the first ½ **mile before turning sharp left and southwards to St Ann's Head.** Westdale Bay, accessible by footpath another ½ mile to the west, is in complete contrast to the sheltered waters of Dale Roads only a mile opposite. This stormy bay, looking straight out to sea, is a good spot for surfing – but not swimming. The Great Castle Headland above is crowned by the impressive remains of an Iron Age promontory fort dating from about 100 BC.

St Ann's Head stands guard over the entrance to the Milford Haven Waterway, a busy shipping route. At the tip of this exposed promontory are a coastguard station, lighthouse and marine rescue centre. In olden days, ships had to make do with a flaming beacon as a warning of the dangerous reefs at the approach to the Haven. The rugged and explosed cliffs around St Ann's Head are noted nesting places for fulmars.

After visiting St Ann's Head, return to Dale, then drive back along the B4327 northwards. Just over 1 mile north of Dale, turn left Ｂ off

---

• PLACES OF INTEREST •

Haverfordwest

Pembrokeshire's old county town is rich in architectural detail. A higgledy-piggledy maze of streets radiates from a hilltop, crowned with the shell of a medieval castle. In town, fine Georgian buildings rub shoulders with modest cottages, while well-planned open spaces contrast with narrow, ancient thoroughfares. Go first to the hilltop for an overview of Haverfordwest and the reasons for its growth. The castle guarded Haverfordwest's location at the highest navigable point on the Western Cleddau, a river which has access to the open seas via the Milford Haven Waterway.

The castle might look in a sorry state today, yet it was sturdy enough to frustrate the demolition team which, under the orders of Oliver Cromwell during the Civil War, failed to raze it to the ground. The ruin shares the hilltop with a squat, sturdy building used in the nineteenth century as a gaol, but now serving as a local government records office.

On the old quayside, warehouses once used to store wool and wine, and an old pub called the Bristol Trader Inn preserve memories of Haverfordwest's strong mercantile links with the West Country. The importance of the town's sea trade led to the mayor also holding the office of Admiral of the Port.

Haverfordwest rewards visitors who enjoy browsing. They will discover historic buildings such as St Mary's Church, which has glorious stained-glass windows, decorative arches and a fifteenth-century oak roof displaying splendid woodcarving, and Castle Square, in the centre of town, a handsome open space lined with tall buildings. On High Street leading upwards from the Square stands the old Shire Hall, an eye-catching neoclassical building dating from 1835. Opposite St Mary's is a strange chamber sunk into the pavement, once used as a crypt, in which bones were stored from an overcrowded churchyard.

Beside the Cleddau at the end of the old quay are the ruins of a medieval priory. Modern Haverfordwest is to be found a little way downriver from the castle, the site of a new waterfront devlopment.

Dale stands in a sheltered spot within the Milford Haven

the B4327 for Marloes. On the approach to Marloes, turn left for Marloes Sands, accessible from the car park 1 mile west of the village. In any survey of the best beaches in Pembrokeshire, Marloes invariably comes at or near the top. You have to make a special effort to get here – which perhaps explains its appeal and unblemished natural beauty. The sandy beach, about ½ mile from the car park, stretches for over a mile below a line of reddish cliffs. At the western end of the beach is Gateholm Island, accessible at low tide, which bears evidence of an ancient settlement where the native Welsh lived during Roman times. For details of the islands – Skomer and Skokholm – visible offshore and accessible from the slipway at Martin's Haven on the western tip of the Marloes Peninsula, please see Places of Interest.

After visiting Marloes, return along the minor road to the B4327, turning left. Turn off the B4327 **C** for Little Haven and Broad Haven (via Talbenny). After Talbenny, the steep, narrow road drops down into Little Haven. This charming spot, a collection of houses perched on a hillside above a small sandy cove, is another place frequented by sailors and windsurfers. Over the headland is bigger brother Broad Haven, still only a smallish resort by the usual standards. The large, gently shelving beach here is superb, but it can become busy at peak weekends. Car parking is good (an excellent information centre on the Pembrokeshire Coast National Park is located in the main parking area).

From Broad Haven, take the B4341 back to Haverfordwest. ■

Marloes' magnificent beach

The Dale Peninsula

This is a place of extremes. It is one of the windiest spots in Britain. Locals have learned to live with over 30 full-scale gales a year, and wind speeds of over 100 mph have been recorded on the peninsula. In compensation, it is also the sunniest place in Wales, with an annual average of over 1,800 hours.

Dale's atmosphere of contented obscurity is captured in this description, taken from a Pembrokeshire guidebook: 'Dale is an Arcadia wherein man's determination turns to water and all good intentions come to nothing.' As with the rest of the Pembrokeshire coast, it is best explored on foot. If you are energetic, you can walk right around the peninsula (a distance of 7 miles), starting and finishing at Dale. For a shorter alternative, park at St Ann's Head and walk along the coast path eastwards to

Mill Bay, where Harri Tudur landed in 1485. Continue along the path to West Blockhouse Point, one of the many fortifications built along the Milford Haven to defend the naval dockyards at Pembroke Dock in the nineteenth century when Britain was gripped by the fear of French invasion. Completed in 1857, West Blockhouse was one of nine forts and gun emplacements completed at that time. Just around the headland is Watwick Bay with its idyllic, golden-sanded beach, one of the loveliest in Pembrokeshire. The distance from St Ann's Head to Watwick Bay, there and back, is about 3 miles.

The Marloes Peninsula and Skomer and Skokholm islands

This promontory juts westwards into the sea from Marloes village. Apart from Marloes Sands, the coastline here is rocky and savage. Just offshore is Skomer Island, a

National Nature Reserve internationally famous as one of the finest sea-bird colonies in North-west Europe. Skomer's populations include fulmars, guillemots, kittiwakes, Manx shearwaters, puffins and razorbills. The island is also an important colony for Atlantic grey seals and home to a unique species of vole.

The smaller island of Skokholm, 2 miles to the south, is another nature reserve of international repute. In 1933, Britain's first bird observatory was established here. Both islands were named by Norse invaders who terrorised the western shores of Wales during the Dark Ages. Skomer, only a mile offshore, is the more accessible of the two. In summer, boat trips to the island run on a regular basis from the slipway at Martin's Haven on the western tip of the Marloes Peninsula.

Little Haven

ST DAVID'S AND NORTH PEMBROKESHIRE

56 MILES – 3 HOURS
START AND FINISH AT HAVERFORDWEST

The stretch of coastline between St David's and Fishguard is, for some, the best part of Pembrokeshire. Well away from the holiday crowds, this rugged, often remote shore has a magnetic appeal. There is also the magic of St David's itself, an ancient site rich in Christian and Celtic heritage. Beach lovers will enjoy superb sands at Newgale and Whitesands Bay, while walkers can follow the coast path past windswept cliffs and crashing seas. This tour is unusually varied: in addition to religious and historic sites, you can also visit a woollen mill, country park and centre for Welsh cheesemaking.

Haverfordwest has a ring-road system that avoids the town centre. **Leave the town on the A487 to St David's. The sea comes spectacularly into view as you drive down into Newgale at the northern end of St Brides Bay.** The expanse of Newgale's west-facing sands is huge, extending for about 2 miles. You can park along the beach by the tall bank of pebbles above the sands and watch the surfers ride the waves.

Next stop is one of the prettiest places in Pembrokeshire. **From Newgale, drive a few miles along the A487 to Solva.**

The miniature port of Lower Solva lies on a sheltered inlet amongst steep folds in the hills, an enclosed spot which seems positively claustrophobic after the wide open spaces of Newgale Sands.

From Solva, continue along the A487 to St David's, Britain's smallest city. The little town, a place of pilgrimage for centuries, grew up around its great cathedral named after Wales's patron saint. St David's stands at the approach to a small peninsula which possesses a compelling beauty and alluring, almost mystical appeal.

On leaving St David's on the A487 to Fishguard, turn left at the outskirts on to the B4583 **A** for a short detour to Whitesands Bay. Even by Pembrokeshire standards, Whitesands is an outstanding beach – with the added advantage of a large, convenient car park. Its sands and rock pools are popular with families, while its west-facing waves attract surfing enthusiasts. The beach nestles beneath rugged St David's Head, a 595-foot high (181 m) promontory rich in ancient sites, including evidence of neolithic and Iron Age settlement.

After visiting Whitesands, return along the B4583 almost all the way to the A487, turning left on to the minor road at the right-hand bend just before the 'B' road meets the 'A' road. Drive along this minor road for about 3 ½ miles until you come to a telephone box. Turn left **B** less than ¼ mile after the telephone box for Abereiddy.

The north Pembrokeshire coast displays a markedly different character to its southern

West-facing Newgale

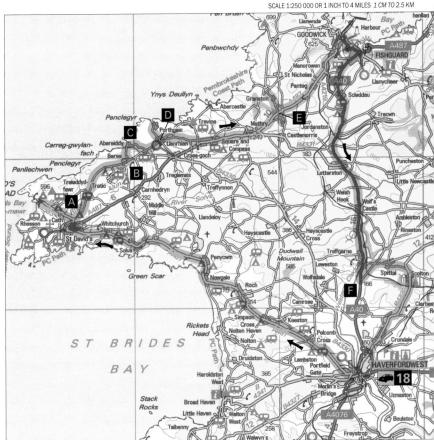

counterpart, a fact nowhere better demonstrated than on this leg of the tour. North Pembrokeshire is rocky and serrated, like the worn teeth of a saw, with few breaks in the cliffs. It is also much remoter than south Pembrokeshire, with nothing like the large concentrations of holiday accommodation available in Tenby or Saundersfoot. Even in the height of summer, it is possible to get away from the crowds here, especially if you take to the coast path.

Abereiddy is a strange but charming place. For a start, it has a beach of blackish sand, caused by the erosion of its slate and shale cliffs. Above the beach are the ruins of workers' cottages, a legacy from the time when the slate was quarried here commercially. Stranger still is the 'blue lagoon' on the headland, a flooded, sheer-sided quarry now

open to the sea. **Leave Abereiddy by the minor road eastwards** C **(not the way you came in), which in 1 mile brings you to a crossroads.**

Turn left here, and in less than a mile you will arrive at Llanrhian. At Llanrhian, turn left at the crossroads D **for a short detour to Porthgain.**

• PLACES OF INTEREST •

Haverfordwest
Please see description in Tour 17.

Solva
The little market town at Lower Solva is one of the safest anchorages in the whole of Pembrokeshire. The picturesque stone quay stands at the head of a narrow inlet protected by steep hills, a good ½ mile from the open sea. Evidence of Solva's past prosperity as a thriving port can be seen in the old lime kilns on the harbours, the large three- and four-storey warehouses close to the quay and the village's grand residences, once owned by prosperous merchants. The harbour was the last sight of Britain for the many nineteenth-century emigrants who paid £3 10 shillings for a passage from Solva to New York. The village is now noted for its excellent choice of high-quality craft shops specialising in clothing, pottery and individual hand-made items. There is an attractive walk from the quayside south along Solva Creek to an Iron Age fort and headland overlooking St Brides Bay.

83

Solva's sheltered harbour

Porthgain is another odd spot which many find strangely seductive. Its snug little harbour is dominated by the remains of a large nineteenth-century crushing plant and other industrial remnants. Until about 150 years ago, Porthgain was an undisturbed backwater, but then quarrying began on the headland above. The local slate and granite were much in demand in Britain's growing industrial towns and cities (Porthgain granite went into the construction of many public buildings in London and Liverpool). Brickmaking and the production of stone chippings for Britain's roads also took place here.

The boom years ended by the start of the 1930s, and today Porthgain is quiet again. Memories of its heyday can be seen in the display of old photographs at the Sloop Inn, a harbourside pub dating from 1743. If you want to see further evidence of Porthgain's industrial past, then follow the coast path west to the headlands where the old quarries and trackways now lie abandoned and silent.

After visiting Porthgain, return to the crossroads, turning left, then in a short distance turn right at the next junction (NB: Do not continue on to Trevine at this junction). In about 1½ miles, this brings you back to the A487, where you turn left towards Fishguard.

At this point E there are two short detours off the A487 (both signposted). To the left, follow the signs for the Tregwynt Woollen Mill, 1½ miles to the north. To the right, follow the signs to the

Llangloffan Farmhouse Cheese Centre, ½ mile to the south.

Tregwynt is a well-known woollen mill which has been working since the eighteenth century (the original water course and wheel which once powered the mill can still be seen). In addition to the mill shop – where a good range of the distinctively patterned cloth typical of the Welsh woollen industry is on sale – visitors can take a tour of the weaving workshops.

Llangloffan is typical of another facet of Welsh rural life – the revival of small cheesemaking enterprises. Wales's speciality cheeses now attract serious praise within the food industry. You can see how it is done at Llangloffan during demonstration sessions (for details telephone 01348 8912441).

After the detours, continue on the A487 via Goodwick to Fishguard. Goodwick, at the northern end of sheltered Fishguard Bay, is a ferry port terminal for Ireland, with ships sailing to Rosslare. The town of Fishguard occupies the headland and small harbour opposite. It is divided into the Upper and Lower Town (the main shopping and commercial area is in the Upper Town, while the Lower Town consists of a picturesque stone quayside, the original harbour on the bay, lined with pretty cottages).

You may want to take a diversion north-westwards from Goodwick through the maze of lanes to Strumble Head on a wild and savage coast. Carregwastad Point, between Goodwick and Strumble Head, features in the history books as the landing place for the last invasion of Britain. This farcical affair took place on 22 February 1797 when a poorly equipped French force, led by an Irish-American general, embarked on a short-lived 'invasion'. They were seen off by the locals, one of whom, Jemima Nicholas, is said to have captured

St David's Cathedral

St David's and peninsula

Faraway St David's and its rock-bound peninsula have always attracted the attentions of the outside world. In the days when it was easier to travel by sea than land, St David's was, in the words of one historian, a 'Piccadilly Circus' of Wales. Early Christian missionaries and pilgrims were attracted to this hallowed spot, Viking plundered the shores, and trading ships called in at Porth Clais, the sheltered port on the peninsula.

The building responsible for St David's city status is not immediately apparent. The cathedral sits hidden away in a steep hollow beneath the streets. Thirty-nine steps lead down to an important Christian shrine, the site of a monastic community founded by Dewi Sant, St David, in the sixth century. The purple-stoned cathedral itself dates from 1176. One of its great glories is its ornately carved fifteenth-century oak roof, a masterpiece of medieval craftsmanship. St David's

status in the medieval church was confirmed by a papal declaration making two pilgrimages to the cathedral equal to one to Rome, and three equal to one to Jerusalem.

Opposite the cathedral stands the Bishop's Palace (Cadw-Welsh Historic Monuments), dating from the thirteenth century. Although now a roofless shell, it still reminds visitors of the wealth – and opulent inclinations – of the medieval church. Open summer daily 9.30–6.30, winter Monday–Saturday 9.30–4, Sunday 2–4. Telephone: (01437) 720517.

From St David's, a number of minor roads radiate out to enchanting spots along the peninsula. A road south-west from St David's leads within a mile to Porth Clais where St David was reputedly baptised. The road due south comes after ½ mile to St Non's Bay, named after the mother of St David. It is said that David was born here during a great storm in about AD 520. A ruined chapel looks out to sea from the

headland, and close by there is a holy well once believed to have miraculous healing powers for eye disease.

The road due west from St David's ends at the cliffs of St Justinian's, where a lifeboat station just about manages to find enough space for itself among the jagged rocks. According to legend, St Justinian, a contemporary of St David, was martyred on Ramsey, the island a short distance offshore. Ramsey is a beautiful spot, a wildlife sanctuary famous for its sea-birds and seals. In the summer, boat trips run to the island from St Justinian's.

The peninsula walk around St David's cannot be too highly recommended. The Pembrokeshire Coast Path winds its way around the indented shoreline with stunning sea views across Ramsey Sound and the open waters of St Brides Bay. If you start at St Justinian's and walk via Porth Clais and St Non's Bay to Caerfai Bay, the one-way distance is 6 ½ miles.

12 Frenchmen single-handed, armed only with a pitchfork! Mementoes of the invasion can be seen in the Royal Oak Inn in the Upper Town. The grave of the formidable Jemima Nicholas is in St Mary's Church.

Leave Fishguard by the A40 south towards Haverfordwest. This road runs through 'Landsker' country, named after the ghostly border – you will not find it on any map – that divides traditionally Welsh north Pembrokeshire from the 'Little England beyond Wales's in the south. For more details on the Landsker, please see the route description in Tour 20.

Turn left ▣ off the A40 by the Corner Piece pub for Scolton Manor Country Park (signposted). In 1 mile, turn right at the crossroads for Spittal, then follow the road through the village for 1 ½ miles, turning right again at

the B4329. The entrance to Scolton Manor Country Park is shortly on the right. The country park, based around a late Georgian mansion built in 1840, has open-air and indoor attractions. The museum here covers wide-ranging themes based on Pembrokeshire's past, including rural and railway

history and archaeology. There is also a countryside centre, based on the varied habitats of the 40-acre (16-hectare) park, a beautiful area of grassland and woodland which can be explored by nature trail.

From Scolton Manor, return along the B4329 to Haverfordwest. ■

St Justinian's lifeboat station on St David's Peninsula

THE PRESELI HILLS AND BEYOND

START AND FINISH AT FISHGUARD
49 MILES – 2 ½ HOURS

The Preseli Hills are Pembrokeshire's only real highlands. Their airy, open flanks, liberally dotted with prehistoric sites, have an eerie atmosphere. This tour takes you to some secretive places – the hidden Gwaun Valley and a churchyard with an ancient cross and 'bleeding' yew tree. In contrast, you will also come across one of Wales's most famous prehistoric sites and a romantic castle which has been a part of the 'Grand Tour' of Wales for centuries. The final leg runs along Pembrokeshire's beautiful coastline. Stop off for the sands at Newport, or take a walk around the spectacular cliffs of Dinas Head.

Fishguard's Welsh name is *Abergwaun,* 'The Mouth of the Gwaun'. The River Gwaun runs through a narrow valley to meet the sea at the picturesque harbour of Lower Fishguard, which was used as the set for the film of Dylan Thomas's *Under Milk Wood* in the early 1970s starring Elizabeth Taylor and Richard Burton. For a fuller description of Fishguard, please see the route details in Tour 18.

From Fishguard, take the B4313 south-east to the Gwaun Valley and Maenclochog. At the right-hand bend on the B4313 about 3 miles from the centre of Fishguard A, take the minor road straight on for Pontfaen and the Gwaun Valley.

Pembrokeshire's coast seems a million miles away from this hidden, sparsely populated valley cloaked in ancient oakwoods. The Gwaun Valley is truly a place apart. When Britain adopted changes to the calendar in 1752, the news may not have filtered through to the residents of the Gwaun Valley. Whatever the reason, the locals still stick to the

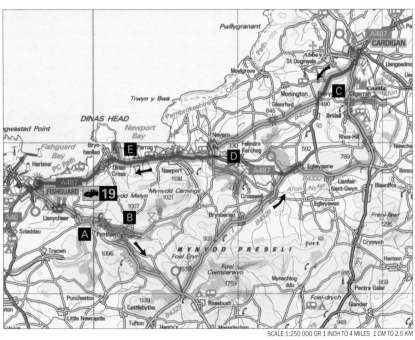

SCALE 1:250 000 OR 1 INCH TO 4 MILES 1 CM TO 2.5 KM

Fishguard, a safe haven on the rocky north Pembrokshire coast

the next junction (in ¼ mile) to rejoin the B4313, where you turn left. Continue along the B4313 to its crossroads with the B4329, turning left here. Up until now, you have been skirting the edge of the Preseli Hills. From the crossroads the road runs through the Preselis, shortly passing through the Cerrig Lladron on your left, an outcrop which rises to 1,535 feet (468 m).

The Preseli Hills are the only part of the Pembrokeshire Coast National Park where the park's boundary ventures inland for any significant distance. Most of the national park hugs the coast in a narrow band; only in the Preselis does it dip inland for about 10 miles to encompass a brooding, treeless range of hills, rising to 1,759 feet (536 m), the bare flanks of which are scattered with a rich picking of mysterious prehistoric sites. Preseli's standing stones, stone circles,

old system at the turn of the year, celebrating New Year's Day on 13 January the traditional way with a meal of goose and plum pudding while the children collect

calennig, gifts of money, apples and oranges.

Turn right in the middle of Pontfaen B across the bridge, bearing right again at

---

• PLACES OF INTEREST •

Welsh Wildlife Centre, near Cilgerran
This large nature reserve covers some 350 acres (141 hectares) and includes a variety of habitats, with wetlands, woodlands, river and meadow. There are hides throughout the reserve, footpaths through one of the largest reed beds in Wales and an 'Animal Kingdom' exhibition covering the period from dinosaurs to the present day. Other attractions include a craft workshop. The reserve is managed by the Dyfed Wildlife Trust. Open daily 10 until dusk (visitor centre closes at 5.30). Telephone: (01239) 621600.

Cilgerran Castle
This beautifully located castle is perched on a crag overlooking the deep and wooded Cilgerran Gorge carved by the River Teifi. Cilgerran was important strategically as the tidal limit of the Teifi, allowing large ships to dock here. It was also the lowest crossing place on

the river at all states of the tide. The stronghold dates from Norman times, though the original fortification here was probably built of wood and timber. The impressive stone defences we see today – most notably the powerful towers – date from the thirteenth century and the time of the castle's recapture from the Welsh by Norman Lord William Marshall the Younger.

Cilgerran had a turbulent history. Its romantic air is partly

based on the story of Nest, the beautiful 'Helen of Wales' who captured the hearts of both Norman nobility and Welsh princes. The story goes that Owain, son of a prince of Powys, abducted Nest, wife of Gerald of Windsor, from Cilgerran Castle in the early twelfth century.

The ruins undoubtedly appeal to the imagination; the castle has been popular with visitors since the earliest days of tourism, and have attracted landscape artists of the stature of JMW Turner and Richard Wilson. One Victorian writer was so overcome by the place that he allowed his imagination – and pen – to run riot, describing Cilgerran thus: 'Looking from this lofty ruin on the embowered glen below one wonders how the passions of war could rage amid such loveliness.' They do not write them like that any more! Open summer daily 9.30–6.30, winter Monday–Saturday 9.30–4, Sunday 2–4. Telephone: (01239) 615136.

The Preseli Hills are scattered with prehistoric sites

burial chambers and cairns – one of the largest concentrations of prehistoric sites in Britain – give rise to much speculation, not least the area's links with Stonehenge (see Pentre Ifan Cromlech in Places of Interest).

Stay on the B4329 through Crosswell to the A487, turning right here in the direction of Cardigan. In about ½ mile you will come to Eglwyswrw. Turn right here on to the B4332. This road brings you to the A478, where you turn left for Cardigan.

At Pen-y-bryn, **turn right off the A478 for a short detour to the Welsh Wildlife Centre and Cilgerran Castle (Cadw-Welsh Historic Monuments).** Cilgerran is attractively located above a spectacular gorge in the River Teifi. You can sometimes see the ancient fishing boats known as coracles in action on the Teifi's waters around Cilgerran. The village holds a Coracle Regatta each summer (for more details on coracles please see Tour 14). **After visiting the wildlife**

centre and castle return to the A478 and continue northwards to Cardigan (the town is by-passed, so you will have to leave the 'A' road to visit it). Leave Cardigan by the A487 westbound to Fishguard. In about 2½ miles after the roundabout on the southern outskirts of Cardigan, turn right on to the B4582 for Nevern. The village has a sympathetically restored medieval church on the site of a religious settlement founded in the sixth century by St Brynach, a Christian missionary from Ireland. But the main source of interest here is a Celtic cross in the churchyard. About 1,000 years old and decorated with an astonishingly complex pattern of carvings, it is one of the finest in Wales. The churchyard also contains an ancient yew tree which is said to 'bleed'.

Leave Nevern by the B4582 south. Where the 'B' road meets the A487, go straight across the 'A' road on to the minor road for a detour to Pentre Ifan Cromlech (Cadw-Welsh Historic Monuments).

The hidden Gwaun Valley

The coast at Dinas Head

Cardigan
Please see description in Tour 14.

Pentre Ifan Cromlech, near Newport
Pentre Ifan, on the northern flanks of the Preseli Hills, is the most-photographed prehistoric monument in Wales. As we see it today, Pentre Ifan reveals the stone foundations of a neolithic chamber built over 5,500 years ago for the communal burial of the dead. The core of the

chamber is created by a massive 16-foot-long (5 m) capstone, balancing on three uprights. Originally, the entire structure would have been covered by an earthen mound.

Sites like Pentre Ifan evoke a sense of mystery and wonderment, especially when you discover that this particular cromlech is made of the same Preseli 'bluestones' which were also used in the construction of Stonehenge's inner circle. No one has yet adequately explained how our ancestors managed to move huge blocks of stone about 200 miles from the far south-west of Wales to Salisbury Plain. Some suggest rafts and boats, others sledges under which logs were placed to act as rollers. Whatever the means of transport, it must have been a truly monumental endeavour.

The monument is signposted from here, but the directions are as follows. In under ½ mile, turn left at the crossroads. In a further 1 ¼ miles turn right and shortly right again. Pentre Ifan is on your right in about ¾ mile. **After visiting Pentre Ifan, return to the A487, turning left for Newport.**

Newport, at the mouth of the River Nevern, is a popular little holiday centre with an excellent sandy beach. It is an attractive, cheerful place, with a good selection of places to stay and eat. The town has a long history, with a charter dating back to the thirteenth century. The castle site (in private ownership) also dates from Norman times. The past is revisited at the town on the third Friday in August when the local inhabitants, on foot and horseback, meet at Newport Square to commence the 'Beating of the Bounds', an ancient custom which served to mark and reinforce local borders.

The skyline above the town is dominated by the rocky ridge of

Carningli Common, which rises to 1,138 feet (350 m). The views from the Iron Age hillfort on the summit, overlooking Newport Bay and the Preseli Hills, are spectacular.

Leave Newport on the A487 westbound. In about 2 ½ miles, turn right off the A487 E for a short detour to Cwm-yr-Eglwys and Dinas Head.
Cwm-yr-Eglwys is a coastal hamlet on the southern approach to the stubby little promontory of Dinas

Head, or Dinas 'Island' (thousands of years ago it was cut off from the mainland but is now connected by a low-lying valley). In October 1859 a huge storm swept ashore and wrecked Cwm-yr-Eglwys's medieval church. Only the belfry and part of the walls survive of a religious site dedicated to St Brynach.

Walkers can follow a magnificent circular coast path from Cwm-yr-Eglwys around Dinas Head, passing the bird colonies on Needle Rock and calling in for some well-deserved refreshment at the unusually named Sailors' Safety Inn on the opposite side of the promontory, before returning along the valley to the starting point. The total distance is just over 3 miles.

Return to the A487, turning right for Fishguard. ■

The attractive little resort of Newport

PEMBROKESHIRE FROM SOUTH TO NORTH

**44 MILES (88 MILES ROUND TRIP) – 2 ½ HOURS (5 HOURS ROUND TRIP)
START AT TENBY, FINISH AT FISHGUARD**

This part of Wales is mostly visited for its coastline. But there is also much to see inland, even though Pembrokeshire's countryside cannot begin to rival its incomparable coastline. This tour cuts straight across country, taking in a varied range of attractions and historic sites. Most interesting of all is the comparison the route affords between south and north Pembrokeshire, the former bearing plentiful evidence of outside influences, the latter maintaining a firmly Welsh identity. This is one of only two linear tours in the book.

Take the A478 north from Tenby. Continue straight on at the large roundabout at Kilgetty, in a mile or so passing the entrance on your left to Folly Farm, a popular tourist attraction. (For details of places to visit on or close to this section of the route – Saundersfoot and Folly Farm in particular – please see Tour 13.)

At Templeton, turn left on to the A4115, and in under 3 miles, turn right on to the A4075. Suddenly, placid

---

Canaston Centre, near Narberth
This indoor attraction brings together a mixed choice of entertainments, including 10-pin bowling, 'Crystal Maze' and adventure games room, designed to appeal to all the family. Open daily 10am–11pm. Telephone: (01834) 891622.

Oakwood Park, near Narberth
If you have children on board, and you have managed to convince them that stopping off at the Canaston Centre is best left to another day, they will certainly not let you pass the entrance to this major Pembrokeshire attraction. Oakwood Park is Wales's answer to Disneyland. Although not on quite the scale of its American harbinger, Oakwood covers a lot of ground – 80 acres (32 hectares) to be precise – and is packed with rides, amusements and entertainments. Like Disney, you pay one admission charge on

entry, which entitles you to unlimited use of the many rides. Do not think you can cover Wales's largest theme park in an hour or so: Oakwood is a day-out destination in the literal sense of the description. Open April–October daily 10–5 (10–10 in August). Telephone: (01834) 891376.

Llawhaden Castle
The prelates of the medieval church were wealthy, worldly men. Llawhaden's impressive ruins began life as a fortification of the bishops of St David's, built on an outcrop above the Eastern Cleddau overlooking some of their richest estates. Over the next few centuries it evolved into something much more welcoming than a draughty castle – a fortified mansion designed as a comfortable medieval house. There are the remains of a great hall, private apartments, decorative archways, kitchens and a bakehouse, along

with defensive features such as a twin-towered gatehouse, which still stands to its full height. By the sixteenth century the bishops had largely abandoned Llawhaden, moving on to the greener pastures of Abergwili near Carmarthen (see Carmarthen Museum entry, Tour 11). Free access.

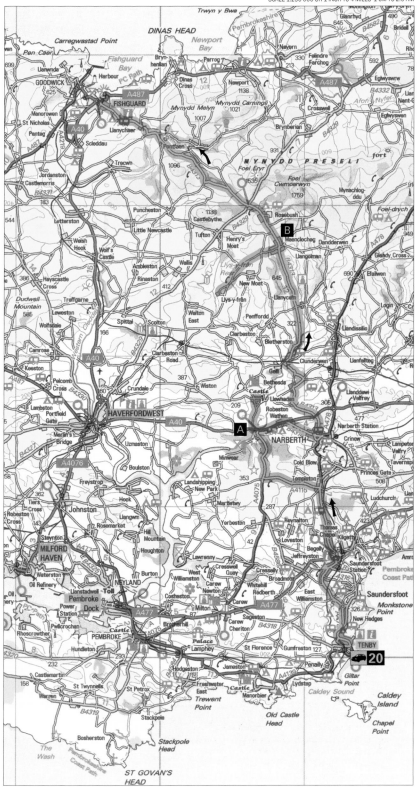

• PLACES OF INTEREST •

Llys-y-frân Country Park

This country park is based around a large reservoir which was built in the early 1970s. A 100-foot-high (30 m) dam holds back the waters of the River Syfynwy, a tributary of the Eastern Cleddau, creating a beautiful 187-acre (76-hectare) lake which has a water-storage capacity of around 2,000 million gallons (9,000 million litres). The purpose-built visitor centre with exhibition area supplies useful information on the many activities that are available. Fishing for rainbow and brown trout is a main attraction (rods are available for hire), and the lake is an ideal venue for

boardsailing, canoeing and dinghy sailing.

Many visitors enjoy the 7 ½-mile perimeter walk, or the two shorter nature trails. The countryside around the reservoir consists of low hills partially clothed with oak and conifer woodland, a mixed habitat which supports a thriving wildlife. Llys-y-frân, named after the nearby village, means 'Court of Crows'. Many birds of the crow family are in evidence, together with sparrowhawks, buzzards, woodpeckers, jays, nuthatches and goldcrests. Open daily 8–dusk. Telephone: (01437) 532273.

Pembrokeshire begins to rival big-time Blackpool as you pass the entrances to two major tourist attractions. **On the junction of the A4115 and A4075 is the Canaston Centre. Turn right here, and shortly you will come to the entrance to Oakwood Park, one of Wales's most popular attractions.**

From Oakwood Park, continue northwards along the A4075 to the A40 at Canaston Bridge. Just before the junction of these two main roads, you can take a short detour left for just under a mile along the minor road to

Blackpool Mill. This handsome four-storey mill was built in the early nineteenth century to grind wheat. It stands amongst woodlands on the upper reaches of the Eastern Cleddau river. Restored machinery shows how the mill used to operate, originally by water power and then turbine. The mill's basement caverns have been converted into an exhibition area featuring extinct wild animals from Wales including, somewhat fancifully, a Welsh dragon.

Turn left on to the A40 and in a very short distance turn right 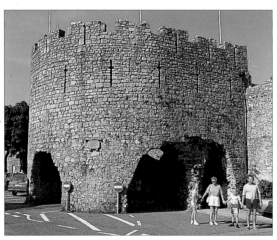 on to the minor road

northwards for a short detour to Llawhaden Castle (Cadw-Welsh Historic Monuments). From its lofty perch, Llawhaden overlooks a patchwork of fields and hills which bears no physical evidence of any kind of boundary. Yet if you look on a detailed map of the area you will see immediate differences. Just to the south of Llawhaden, for example, are English-sounding place-names such as Robeston Wathen and Coxlake. A few miles to the north are quintessentially Welsh places like Llandissilio and Llanycefn.

The difference is explained by the Landsker (or land-scar), an imaginary line running across Pembrokeshire from Amroth to Newgale. Marked by a series of castles, now mostly ruined, it effectively cuts Pembrokeshire in two.

The Normans established a frontier of castles beyond which the Welsh retreated to the north. In the wake of the invaders came English and Flemish immigrants and a south Pembrokeshire 'Little England' of imported ways, customs, farming methods, architecture and alien place-names. Over the centuries, the Landsker's relevance inevitably declined, though not so long ago intermarriage between families on

Five Arches, Tenby

either side of the border was actively discouraged.

After visiting Llawhaden, return to the A40, turning left. At Robeston Wathen, turn right on to the B4314 for Narberth. There is more history to delve into in the pleasant country town of Narberth. It was one of the homes of the princes of Dyfed, and is mentioned in the *Mabinogion*, a collection of early Welsh folk tales. The Wilson Museum displays an engaging array of local items which illustrate life in Narberth over the centuries. The building in which the museum is housed is itself noteworthy, for it preserves part of an old pub. Ruined Narberth Castle, built on the Landsker just south of the town centre, is in private ownership.

Just south-west of the town is Heron's Brook Country Park and Waterfowl Centre, another of the attractions which has grown up to serve south Pembrokeshire's many summer holidaymakers. Ducks and geese from all over the world can be seen here, together with farm animals, rare breeds and ponies. The park also has a woodland walk and many picturesque picnic areas.

Leave Narberth by the B4313 northwards. Cross the A40, staying on the B4313 northwards to Maenclochog. At Maenclochog, take a detour off the B4313 for Llys-y-frân Country Park. Turn left at the village **B** **then go straight along the minor road for just over 3 miles to the country park.** Llys-y-frân, located in the green heart of Pembrokeshire, offers a well-developed range of leisure

pursuits. **After visiting the country park, retrace your steps to Maenclochog and join the B4313 northwards, which takes you to the tour's end at Fishguard.** For the latter part of the tour, you will be running along the western flank of Pembrokeshire's Preseli Hills, close to the Gwaun Valley (for details, see Tour 19, which shares a common route – but in reverse – most of the way back to Fishguard). ■

Waterfall ride, Oakwood Park

93

USEFUL ADDRESSES AND INFORMATION

Tourist Information Centres

Normal opening times are 10am–5.30pm. These hours may vary to suit local circumstances. Those marked with an asterisk (*) are open seasonally only (April–September).

Abergavenny
Swan Meadow, Monmouth Road, Abergavenny NP7 5HH
Tel: (01873) 857588

Barry Island *
The Triangle, Paget Road, Barry Island CF62 8TJ
Tel: (01446) 747171

Brecon
Cattle Market Car Park, Brecon LD3 9DA
Tel: (01874) 622485

Caerleon
High Street, Caerleon
Tel: (01633) 422656

Caerphilly
Lower Twyn Square, Caerphilly CF83 1XX
Tel: (01222) 851378

Cardiff
Central Station, Cardiff CF1 1QY
Tel: (01222) 227281

Cardigan
Theatr Mwldan, Bath House Road, Cardigan SA43 2JY
Tel: (01239) 613230

Carmarthen
Lammas Street, Carmarthen SA31 3AQ
Tel: (01267) 231557

Chepstow
Castle Car Park, Bridge Street, Chepstow NP6 5EY
Tel: (01291) 623772

Crickhowell *
Beaufort Chambers, Beaufort Street, Crickhowell NP8 1AA
Tel: (01873) 812105

Cwmcarn
Visitor Centre, Cwmcarn Forest Drive, nr Cross Keys NP1 7FA
Tel: (01495) 272001

Fishguard Harbour
Passenger Concourse, The Harbour, Goodwick, Fishguard SA64 0BU
Tel: (01348) 872037

Fishguard Town
4 Hamilton Street, Fishguard SA65 9HL
Tel: (01348) 873484

Haverfordwest
Old Bridge, Haverfordwest SA61 2EZ
Tel: (01437) 763110

Kilgetty *
Kingsmoor Common, Kilgetty SA68 0YA
Tel: (01834) 813672

Llandarcy *
BP Club, Llandarcy, Neath SA10 6HJ
Tel: (01792) 813030

Llandovery *
Central Car Park, Broad Street, Llandovery SA20 0AR
Tel: (01550) 720693

Llanelli
Public Library, Vaughan Street, Llanelli SA15 3AS
Tel: (01554) 772020

Magor
Granada Services West, Junction 23 M4, Magor NP6 3YL
Tel: (01633) 881122

Merthyr Tydfil
14a Glebeland Street, Merthyr Tydfil CF47 8AU
Tel: (01685) 379884

Milford Haven *
94 Charles Street, Milford Haven SA73 2HL
Tel: (01646) 690866

Monmouth *
Shire Hall, Agincourt Square, Monmouth NP5 3DY
Tel: (01600) 713899

Mumbles *
Oystermouth Square, Mumbles, Swansea SA3 4DQ
Tel: (01792) 361302

Narberth
Town Hall, Narberth SA67 7AR
Tel: (01834) 860061

Newcastle Emlyn *
Market Hall, Newcastle Emlyn SA38 9AE
Tel: (01239) 711333

Newport
Newport Museum and Art Gallery, John Frost Square, Newport NP9 1HZ
Tel: (01633) 842962

Pembroke
Visitor Centre, Commons Road, Pembroke SA71 4EA
Tel: (01646) 622388

Pembroke Dock *
The Gun Tower, Front Street, Pembroke SA72 6JX
Tel: (01646) 622246

Penarth *
Penarth Pier, The Esplanade, Penarth CF64 3AU
Tel: (01222) 708849

Pont Abraham
Pont Abraham Services, Junction 49 M4, Llanedi SA4 1FP
Tel: (01792) 883838

Pont Nedd Fechan
nr Glyn Neath SA11 5NR
Tel: (01639) 721795

Pontypridd
Historical and Cultural Centre, The Old Bridge, Pontypridd CF37 3PE
Tel: (01443) 409512

Porthcawl
Old Police Station, John Street, Porthcawl CF36 3DT
Tel: (01656) 786639

St David's *
City Hall, St David's SA62 6SD
Tel: (01437) 720392

Sarn
Sarn Park Services, Junction 36 M4, nr Bridgend CF32 9SY
Tel: (01656) 654906

Swansea
PO Box 59, Singleton Street, Swansea SA1 3QG
Tel: (01792) 468321

Tenby
The Croft, Tenby SA70 8AP
Tel: (01834) 842402

Other useful organisations

Brecon Beacons National Park
Park Office, 7 Glamorgan Street, Brecon LD3 7DP
Tel: (01874) 624437

Pembrokeshire Coast National Park
National Park Department, County Offices, St Thomas Green, Haverfordwest SA61 1QZ
Tel: (01437) 764591

Ordnance Survey
Romsey Road, Maybush, Southampton SO16 4GU
Tel: 0345 330011 (Lo-call)

Wales Tourist Board
Davis Street, Cardiff CF1 2FU
Tel: (01222) 475226